PRACTICAL SEAMANSHIP

.....how to handle your boat like a pro.

DAVID S. YETMAN

Editor: Phyllis Klucinec

BRISTOL FASHION PUBLICATIONS, INC.
Harrisburg, Pennsylvania

Practical Seamanship -- *David S. Yetman*

Published by Bristol Fashion Publications, Inc.

ISBN: 1-892216-37-X
LCCN: 2001-131234

Contribution acknowledgments

Inside Graphics: David S. Yetman.
Cover Design: David S. Yetman
Cover Photography: David S. Yetman
Cover Model: Patricia Quinn Yetman

To my ever-patient, indispensable
First Mate, Pat

FOREWORD

As TechStar *approached the marina, her skipper did a careful visual check of the traffic conditions in the harbor, then reached over to the mouse in the navigation station and used it to select the* docking *icon on the computer display. Satisfied that his selection had registered, he turned and walked back to the cockpit to join his guests as the boat continued toward shore.*

The navigational computer responded by tapping into the data bus that linked all of the boat's instruments and began gathering information in preparation for docking. Radar reported no traffic in the way; the GPS verified the location; analysis of the video images of the dock indicated that the space was clear and the weather station on the mast chimed in with wind speed and direction data. The computer instructed the engine controllers to reduce the boat's forward speed; it adjusted the rudders' angle to compensate for the current in the outgoing tide, then began to pulse the bow and stern thrusters on and off to position the boat in proper alignment as it neared the dock. After a nearly imperceptible application of reverse thrust brought the boat to a stop, a muted alarm sounded to alert the skipper that it was time to drop the fenders into position and secure the dock lines. Until he did, the computer held the boat in position - two feet from the dock face - based on the input from a series of tiny sonar transducers which transmitted distance information from their position along the vessel's waterline.

That description of automated docking may seem like science fiction, but it is fiction only because no one has bothered to do it yet. The good news is that all of the technologies already exist and it is only a matter of time until someone puts them all together on a boat. The bad news is that the first implementation will, almost certainly, be on a high-priced megayacht and it will be years before the cost of the technology comes down to the point where it is affordable for smaller boats. Until then, boat owners will have to continue to wrestle with wind, tide and the uncertainties of handling boats as they always have.

Seamanship encompasses many skills and activities. It includes knowledge of piloting, navigation, lines and knots, weather wisdom, communication and maintenance, much of which is acquired through experience and, therefore, difficult to teach in a tutorial. Knowledge about another important aspect of seamanship - boat handling - is also experience-based, but learning it can be helped considerably by an understanding of how the boat and its systems work. That is where *Practical Seamanship* comes in.

Practical seamanship – handling a boat at slower speeds - especially in tight quarters or in adverse conditions, is a skill that separates the tyros from the pros. Its challenges are such that even the most experienced skipper can run into problems or get embarrassed on occasion. I was on the Casco Bay ferry, *ISLAND HOLIDAY*, a couple of years ago as it approached the dock at Little Diamond Island, Maine, one of the many stops on its route. The captain had, obviously, misjudged the conditions, because he came in so fast even a last-minute application of full-throttle power in reverse couldn't prevent a jarring collision that rattled the wooden pier and nearly toppled the passengers waiting there. Fortunately, the only damage was to the captain's ego, so I can admit that I derived some satisfaction from his error. If a pro, who had stopped at that same dock hundreds of times, could have such a problem, then I shouldn't feel badly about entertaining the locals with an occasionally, inelegant approach of my own.

The information in *Practical Seamanship* will not guarantee that you will never suffer the embarrassment of a misjudged docking attempt, but it will provide you with an understanding of the forces at work, how different propulsion systems affect your ability to maneuver the boat and how you can use their capabilities to your advantage. There are separate sections on single-screw inboard and twin-screw boats that outline areas where their performance differs from outboard or stern-drive boats (which, together, comprise the majority of pleasure craft in use today). In all cases, the emphasis is on slow-speed handling, docking - both coming and going, anchoring and things to look out for while under way.

Practical Seamanship is based on the hard-won practical experience of someone who has made far more than his share of boat-handling errors along the way - some comical, some not. I hope it will help you avoid a few of your own.

My thanks to Newport's (formerly Newburyport's) Dick Fredrickson for his thoughtful review of my manuscript.

DSY

TABLE OF CONTENTS

Chapter 1
HANDLING & MANEUVERABILITY

Someone once characterized handling a boat as "driving a car with no brakes on a moving icy road". It may not be quite that bad, but it is true you cannot maneuver a boat with the surety or accuracy of driving a car. The car has a relatively firm grip on the road surface, a responsive speed control, brakes and a steering system that is almost second-nature to people from the industrialized world. You can drive with the assurance that the front end will go precisely where you steer the front wheels and the rear wheels will obediently follow closely in their tracks. When you stop, the car stays stopped and there is no need to tie it to a stationary object when you park.

Not so, in a boat. To begin with, it steers from the back, so the orientation of the bow is only indirectly controlled by the action of the rudder. When you turn the wheel to port, the stern moves to starboard. Other than reversing the direction of thrust, there is no way to stop the boat, and shutting the engine off or putting it in neutral doesn't, necessarily, mean it will stop moving. I can still remember how astounded I was when I launched my first boat and realized how little control I could exercise over its direction during docking maneuvers. I had taken an eight-session Coast Guard Auxiliary course and read everything I could get my hands on, but I was still unprepared for anything but *you turn the wheel and the boat goes where you point it.*

At least some of the difficulty experienced by beginning boaters can be traced to a lack of familiarity with the mechanics of steering a boat. My own difficulties continued as long as I insisted on thinking about how my steering input was going to control the bow. They began to abate as soon as I started thinking in terms of how my input was going to affect the *stern*, where the steering is, and how that, in turn, would affect the bow. From that point on, I had a much better picture of what I had to do to coax the boat onto the intended course. 1616

I also had to learn where the boat's turning axis was Returning to the automotive analogy; turning the steering wheel results in a predictable change in the direction of the front of a car. In the case of a boat, turning the wheel results in the stern going one way and the bow in the other – and the two movements are not always equal. One of the reasons for the discrepancy is the boat's turning axis - which is generally located at the hull's point of greatest resistance to turning. This point may not be where you would expect it to be.

Figure 1 shows three examples of steering axis locations, the position of which are marked by a circle of arrows, (this format is used to illustrate pivot points throughout this book). If the boat has a deep forefoot or a load concentrated forward (1) its turning axis would be forward of center. It would result in unequal movement, where the stern swings further than the bow (as shown by the broken line outline). A boat whose load is concentrated aft (2) would behave in the opposite manner, because its turning axis would be aft of midships. The turning axis of a sailboat with a substantial ballast keel (3) would be amidships, causing it to exhibit nearly equal movement of bow and stern – the reason many of them can turn on a dime.

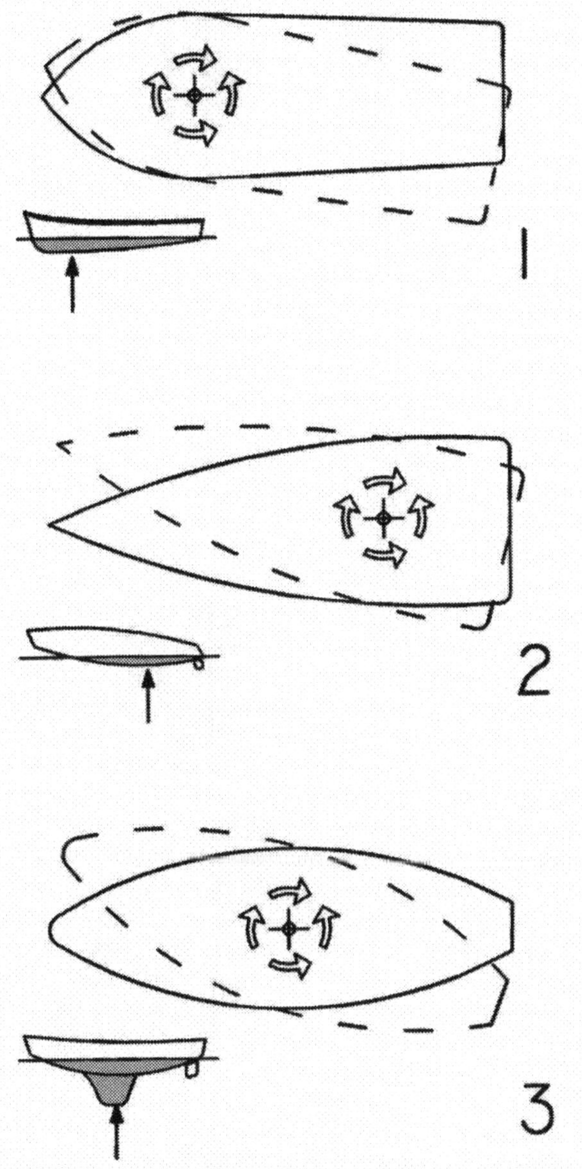

Figure 1

Position of turning axis in various hull types

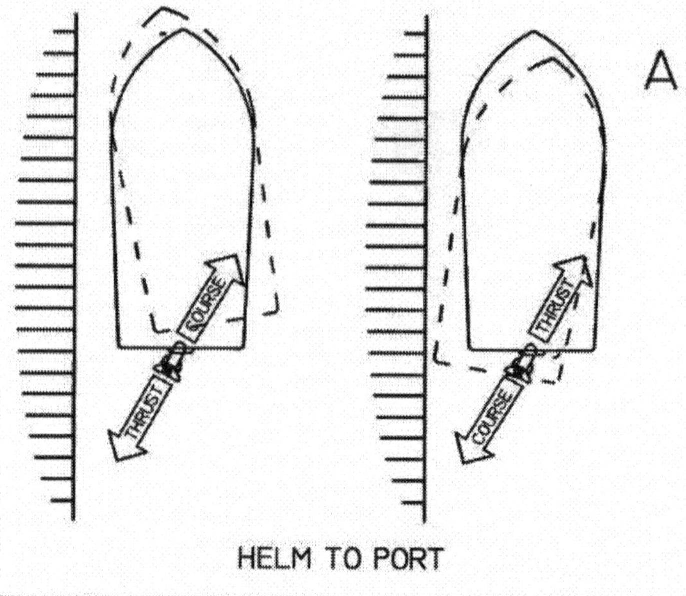

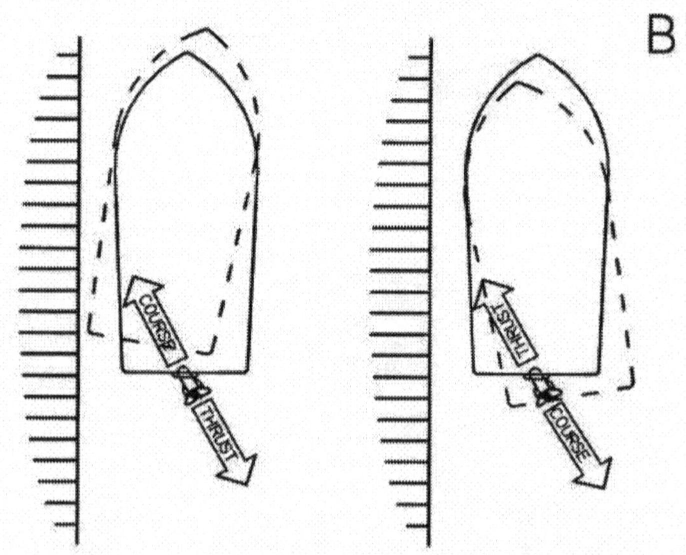

Figure 2

Angles of thrust at various rudder positions

Other aspects boaters often neglect to consider are the different angles of thrust that result from various outdrive or outboard positions. As an example, use the boat in Figure 2 with the dock on its port side. When the wheel is turned to port, as shown in Panel A, the outdrive or outboard will swing in that direction. When forward gear is engaged, the stern will move ahead and to starboard. In reverse, it will pull the stern closer to the dock on the port side.

If the wheel is turned to starboard in the same situation (Panel B), the motions will be reversed. Forward gear will push the stern forward and into the dock. Reverse will pull it away.

While all of these options are useful in the appropriate situation, they are a lot for a novice to remember in the midst of docking a boat, particularly since most of the action takes place behind them. They seem complex at first, but once you learn to visualize what happens in response to your input at the helm, they become instinctive ways for you to control or, at least, influence the course of your boat during slow-speed maneuvers.

Another very useful bit of information that will contribute to your expertise, is being able to relate the position of your rudder to the position of the wheel at the helm. If the total travel of the wheel is 4 turns lock-to-lock, for example, you can assume the rudder is centered (straight ahead) when you have rotated the wheel 2 turns from full lock. In the case of a mechanical steering system, you can mark the top of the wheel with a strip of tape or a few turns of small-diameter line to indicate dead center. The wheel in a hydraulic system is not directly connected to the rudder, so "center" may not always correlate precisely to the same wheel position, but you can still count turns to determine the approximate position. Knowing the position of the rudder is good information to have before you get under way, especially in tight surroundings.

The behavior of a boat and its ease of handling are also affected by external influences like forward speed, wind and current and by a long list of internal (i.e.: onboard) variables such as size, style, hull shape, below-the-waterline characteristics, type of propulsion it uses, the number of motors it has and the placement of its gear and accessories Unless your driving includes Indy or NASCAR events, none of those variables has an appreciable impact on your ability to drive your car well. Every one of them affects the handling of your boat.

Chapter 2
EXTERNAL INFLUENCES

The primary external influences are current and wind Their effect is quite similar, but their force is directed at different parts of the boat The force of current is applied to the part of the boat below the waterline. Wind affects only the part above. The impact of either one depends on how much resistance the size and shape of your boat present to them The boats shown in Figure 3 are good examples of the difference The top boat is a low, open launch with a deep forefoot and a substantial keel Because of the relatively large area presented by its underbody, it would be strongly affected by current coming at an angle to the bow, but would be only slightly affected by wind from the same direction, since its low profile presents little resistance. (In discussions like this one, the profile of a boat is often referred to as *windage*). The keel would also increase its tendency to stay on a straight course while underway.

The lower boat, a modern, high-sided cabin cruiser, would not be as affected by current, since a relatively small portion of its structure is below the waterline It would, however, be drastically affected by a beam wind, because its windage presents so much resistance and there is so little below the waterline to counteract the movement The relatively small proportion of its structure below the waterline could also detract from its tracking ability in breezy conditions The low-speed handling characteristics of these two boats could hardly be more different, with a definite edge in stability going to the launch.

The effects of current are fairly straightforward If you are running with it, it will enhance your speed Going against it will slow you down. Running at an angle to the flow will tend to push you off-course, forcing you to take corrective measures.

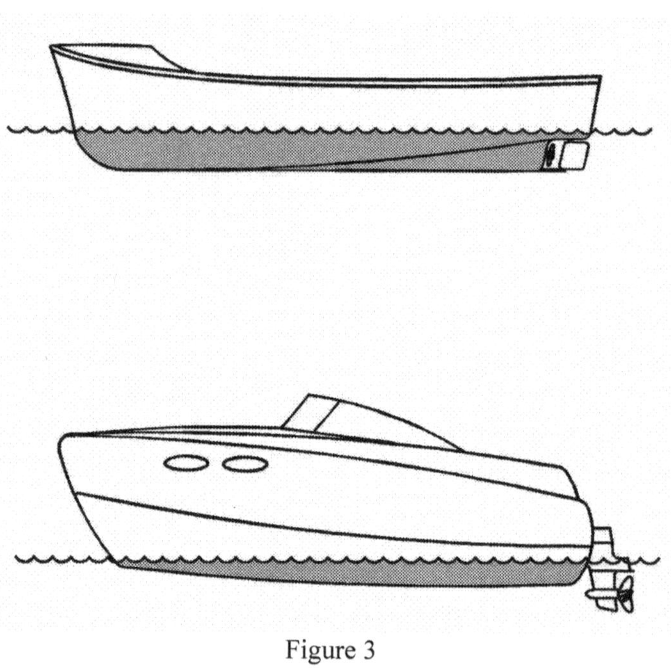

Figure 3

Comparison of windage and underbody features

Current can also have a direct impact on your ability to steer with a rudder. The effectiveness of a rudder increases with the speed of water going past it and is reduced as the water flow slows down. If there is no water moving past the rudder, it has no effect regardless of its position If your true speed over ground is 5 knots and you are heading into a 3-knot current, the water is moving past your rudder at 8 knots, making it fairly easy to control the direction of travel However, if you turn around so the current is flowing with you and maintain your true speed, the speed of the water going past your rudder will be reduced to just 2 knots. This will greatly impair your ability to keep the boat on course.

Currents are not always obvious unless you know what to look for. Watching the behavior of other boats around you is one way to see their influence Looking for tilting buoys is another. Fortunately, most boaters do not have to deal with the strong currents present in some rivers, but even weak currents can be a factor in slow-speed maneuvers such as docking. We will look at that more closely in Chapter 7.

The other external influence on boat handling is wind It results in some of the same effects as current, but unless it is quite strong, the severity of its impact is determined more by the design of the boat than any other factor. A tall, slab-sided boat, such as the one in Figure 3, or a boat with a large canvas enclosure will be drastically affected by wind and can be quite difficult to handle under severe weather conditions In such cases, it pays to keep close tabs on the wind strength and direction and have a complete understanding of how they affect your boat.

Sailors use *telltales*, shorts lengths of fabric attached to the body and edges of sails, to allow them to "see" the wind so they can tell when their sails are trimmed properly. Power boaters need to see the wind too. Knowing how it will affect you as you prepare to approach or leave a dock, or head for a launch ramp can make the difference between an uneventful landing and one you would rather forget You can create a telltale by tying a short length of narrow, brightly colored ribbon tightly around the tip of your VHF antenna leaving the ends free to fly in the wind. If you come to a stop for just a moment before heading in, you'll see exactly where the wind is coming from and how it will affect you

One of the best demonstrations of how different boats are affected by external influences is to observe a group of boats moored in an inlet or harbor as the tide changes on a windy day. If the current and wind are coming from the same direction, all of the boats will be aligned to head into them But if the wind changes and comes in from a different direction, the boats will lose their alignment and begin to point in different directions. Those, such as sailboats, with a substantial underbody or keel will continue to be controlled by the current, while others with greater windage will respond to the wind instead. The rest, whose attributes are more equally balanced, will wander back and forth, following whichever influence happens to be stronger at any given moment.

Chapter 3
ONBOARD INFLUENCES

There are many aspects in design of a boat which can contribute or detract from the skipper's ability to handle it As discussed in the previous chapters, two of them, windage and below-the-waterline features, have a direct connection to the impact of external influences, such as wind and current, on the handling of the boat Others, such as hull shape, weight distribution, helm position and the location of accessories, such as cleats and bitts, have varying degrees of impact that can range from detrimental to just plain inconvenient For the most part, they are built-in aspects of the design, so there is little you can do about them, other than learning how to cope with them effectively.

The most important on-board influence, however, is the boat's propulsion system It is what imparts motion to the boat and motion is what you are trying to control in handling the boat. Propulsion systems have a number of variables, including:

Number of engines:	single, dual
Engine location:	outboard, stern, or amidships
Drive type:	outboard, stern drive, inboard (straight shaft) or water jet
Propeller(s):	single, dual (counter-rotating on concentric shafts)
Other aids:	bow or stern thrusters

Each of the many combinations of the above conditions

has a fairly well-defined position in the ratings when it comes to their contribution to ease of handling. A twin- screw inboard with both bow and stern thrusters may be at the top of the list, but it is a combination rarely seen in pleasure boats and non-existent in mid-size and smaller craft That leaves the top spot open to be shared by a group of boats with very similar handling abilities The group includes boats with twin inboards, twin inboards with jackshafts and outdrives, twin stern drives and, finally, twin outboards, especially if the outboard motors are mounted well aft of the transom on extension brackets The middle of the list is occupied by boats using a single outboard or stern drive for power. A single-screw, straight inboard engine configuration is at the very bottom of nearly everyone's list

It may be premature to try to position water-jet-drive boats on the list Their use in pleasure boats is again on the rise, but the many variations in how they are used makes them difficult to classify. At one end of the spectrum are the installations where the jet drive pump is coupled directly to the engine, meaning that there is no neutral - when the engine is running, you are moving At the extreme opposite end are systems - such as those used by Hinckley, Little Harbor and others - which integrate the directional control of the water jet and a bow thruster in a single joystick Most manufacturers who offer jet-drive boats will admit they take some getting used to.

One obstacle to handling ease present in virtually all boats, is that the bow is the least controllable part of the boat Going forward, the position of the bow can be indirectly controlled by steering with the rudder, but in reverse the bow is reduced to being a trailer, subject to the forces of wind and current. At the same time, the boat is plowing through the water, blunt end (transom) first, so it lacks the directional guidance that the pointed bow normally provides when going forward. As a result, the boat tends to wander and requires a knowledgeable hand at the helm to keep it on course As we will see in Chapter 6, twin screws provide greatly increased control over the bow, going forward or backward, albeit at a considerable mechanical disadvantage.

The real champion of bow control is a bow thruster. Their use was formerly limited to commercial vessels and large pleasure boats, but this has been changing as more manufacturers offer them for smaller, single-screw boats. Two popular manufacturers, Bayliner and Maxum, have recently unveiled systems which offer joy-stick-controlled bow *and* stern thrusters on boats as small as 23 feet. What has been a rare and esoteric accessory for years may finally become the norm, and boat handling will be easier because of it.

Other factors that affect your ability to safely and effectively handle your boat are the availability and location of cleats, chocks and bitts for dock and spring lines. While most people don't include these accessories in any discussion of boat handling, their presence and accessibility can make a real difference in docking operations. How well you use them is also an important consideration that will be addressed in Chapter 7 and beyond.

Chapter 4 SLOW-SPEED MANEUVERING SINGLE-SCREW INBOARD BOATS

Single-screw inboard boats come to mind whenever classic boats are mentioned. The layout has been a mainstay of working vessels – and later, pleasure boats – ever since the modern propeller was developed 150 years ago. Its position as the main form of pleasure boat propulsion began to slip with the introduction of Evinrude's *detachable rowboat motor* in 1909 and declined even further when Volvo introduced the stern drive in 1959. A great majority of pleasure boats now use one of those two propulsion systems. The single-screw inboard is almost everyone's choice as the least manageable propulsion system, but recognizing its weaknesses is key to understanding the mechanics of boat handling and will lead to a fuller appreciation of the capabilities of other types of propulsion.

One of the strengths of an inboard system is its simplicity. The propeller shaft is usually a solid rod that runs straight aft from the transmission and is supported just ahead of the propeller by a Cutless bearing in a strut or a skeg. The propeller turns with the shaft, creating a backwash (thrust) which causes the boat to move, more-or-less, straight ahead or, when reversed, somewhat less straight rearward. The rudder, which is placed directly abaft the propeller, is used to redirect part of the thrust to one side, deflecting the stern of the boat in the opposite direction to initiate a change in course. Keep in mind that the boat moves in the opposite direction of the thrust being produced by its propulsion system. See Figure 4.

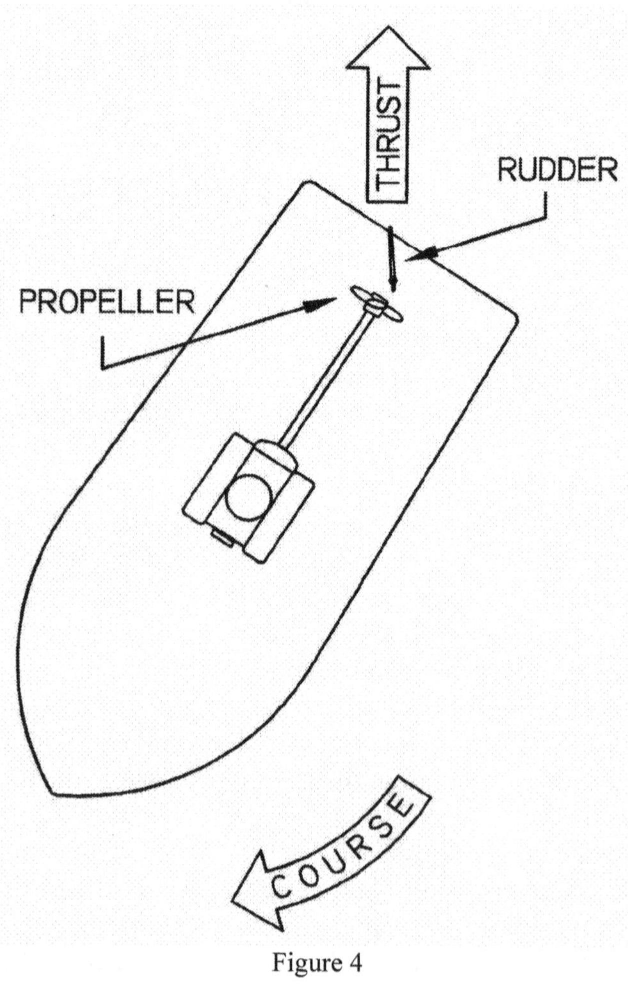

Figure 4

Single-screw inboard propulsion system

There are those who will argue that the water going past the rudder is technically the result of the movement of the boat through the water. That is closer to being true when the boat is at speed. It would be absolutely true if the boat were being towed. But when the boat is accelerating under its own power, the speed of the water being pushed past the rudder (the backwash) is greater than the speed of the boat and provides more effective control than the forward speed of the boat alone would offer.

The system works, but its maneuverability suffers somewhat in comparison to outboards and stern drives because the rudder deflects only part of the thrust, and its effectiveness is reduced even further if the speed of the water going past it slows down. That phenomenon is also a contributing factor to the lack of steering effectiveness in reverse.

Single-screw inboards are notoriously difficult to control in reverse. Part of the difficulty is the comparative lack of water going past the rudder. As shown in Figure 5, the thrust from the propeller goes forward, so the water is being drawn in from areas that bypass the rudder, resulting in less water going past the rudder and a loss of control. This difficulty is compounded by the phenomenon called *propwalk*, where the rotation of the propeller results in a paddlewheel effect that causes the stern to move sideways A propeller that turns clockwise in reverse (as viewed from aft) will cause the stern to walk to starboard. One that turns counterclockwise will move to port. Propwalk is present under all conditions, but is a greater problem in reverse. There are several highly technical explanations for the disparity. The cause of propwalk is often attributed to the downward propeller shaft angle of most inboards, the profile the blades present to the water as a result of the shaft angle and to the greater effectiveness of propeller blades at the bottom of their stroke. Propwalk is also present when going forward, but is less obvious because of greater speeds involved, allowing the rudder to do a better job of compensating for it. Whatever the cause, propwalk is the bane of single-screw skippers who need to back up.

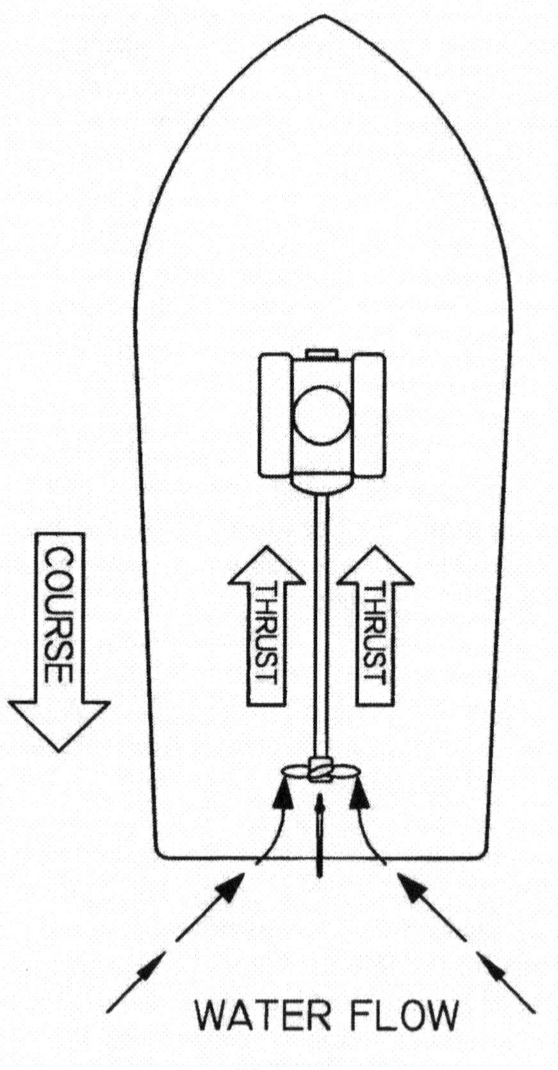

Figure 5

The path of water flowing past the rudder while backing up

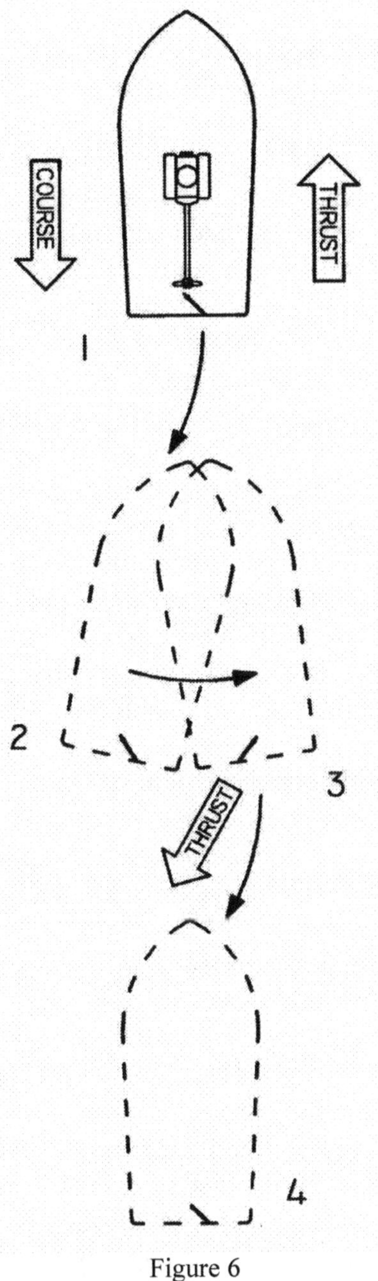

Figure 6

Overcoming propwalk in reverse

A common procedure for backing up over an extended distance is illustrated in Figure 6. With the rudder turned opposite the propwalk to compensate as much as possible, the boat is allowed to travel to the point where it is off the intended course. Then the rudder is turned in the opposite direction and a burst of power is applied in forward gear to push the stern over to the intended course line or beyond. A quick burst is critical, so the stern is pushed to the side before any appreciable forward motion can take place. Then the entire cycle is repeated until the boat has been backed out sufficiently to be turned around for departure.

Another situation where propwalk can be a problem is during docking. If the boat walks to starboard and the dock happens to be on that side, the stern will tuck into the dock nicely when you engage reverse to bring the boat to a halt, making you look like a pro. If the dock is to port, however, you will face the frustrating prospect of having the stern walk away from the dock when you put the boat in reverse. The smart choice is to avoid docking on the unfavorable side. Otherwise, the best way to minimize the problem is to approach the dock as slowly as possible, reducing the amount of reverse power that will be required to stop the boat. In a worst-case scenario, where wind or current add to the problem, there may be no solution other than soliciting the help of someone on the dock to catch a line and pull in the unruly stern.

The use of bow thrusters is an increasingly popular remedy for the handling weaknesses of single-screw inboards. More and more boatbuilders are offering them as an option on boats as small as 28 feet. They are not cheap – they start at around $5,000 – but they are far less expensive than equipping a boat with dual engines, and they provide many of the same benefits. Bow thrusters consist of a small propeller mounted inside an athwartships tunnel through the bow, just below the water line. The propeller is driven by a reversible electric motor which is controlled by a helm-mounted switch. This allows the thrust to be directed from either end of the tunnel and will push the bow one way or the other. The thrusters for larger vessels may have double propellers and are usually hydraulically powered. Strictly for low-speed use, they provide very precise control of the bow - whether the boat is under way or not - and can be used to turn a boat around in not much more than its own length. A skillfully used bow thruster can even be used to steer a boat quite effectively while backing up. It is a maneuver that takes a great deal of practice, but that can be said of most everything associated with handling a single-screw inboard.

Anything considered a classic will always have a following of purists who would not own or use anything else. Single-screw inboard boats are no exception. But after a season or two of wrestling with their peculiarities, even a purist would grow to appreciate the attributes of more manageable alternatives such as outboards, stern drives and, of course, twin screws.

Chapter 5
SLOW-SPEED MANEUVERING SINGLE OUTBOARD OR STERN-DRIVE BOATS

Outboard motors and stern-drive systems are as different as two devices can be. Each has its die-hard proponents, but they share one attribute that puts them very near the top of the list for ease of handling In both systems, the propeller shaft is mounted in a gear housing (the lower unit of an outboard motor or the outdrive section of a stern drive) that can pivot from side-to-side to *direct the propeller's thrust.* It would be difficult to over-emphasize the importance of that feature and the many benefits it offers

The ability to direct the propeller's thrust provides far more precise, directional control than traditional inboard systems. It also eliminates the need for a separate rudder and its steering inefficiencies

The gear housings are shaped to act as a rudder to enhance stability and steering at speed, but they have too little surface area that is flat enough to contribute much to control at low speed. Both systems place the propeller some distance aft of the transom, providing more responsive steering because of the leverage involved

The benefit is particularly apparent in the case of an

outboard motor mounted behind the transom on an extension bracket.

The need for a long propeller shaft to slope upward to make a connection with an inboard engine is eliminated by the right-angle gear system that drives the lower unit's short propeller shaft. This design allows the shaft to be positioned horizontally so the propeller can operate in its most efficient position under all conditions. In a traditional inboard layout, some of the output of the angled propeller is expended trying to push the boat up instead of pushing it forward. The efficiency that results from the horizontal shaft position is the primary reason these systems will outperform an inboard if all other conditions are equal. The part of the propwalk problem attributable to the shaft angle of an inboard system is eliminated and any residual tendency for propwalk is offset by the ability to direct the thrust to compensate for it. Figure 7 is a simplified drawing of outboard and stern-drive gearing paths.

In addition to pivoting from side to side, most outboards and outdrives provide tilt adjustment. This allows the propeller shaft to be angled up or down to bring the boat into proper trim and compensate for various operating conditions and loads. Tilting the angle down, for example, will cause the stern to lift, driving the bow down to slice into a choppy sea rather than bouncing over each wave. The outdrive has an edge over the outboard in this department because it has a greater range of adjustment while still keeping the propeller under water.

Under normal conditions, the absence of shaft angle, the position of the propeller in the water and the shape of the lower unit combine to allow the system to propel the boat almost as well in reverse as it does going forward. Although the blunt end of the boat is still being pushed through the water and the bow is still free to be affected by wind and current, the boat can be steered quite effectively in reverse.

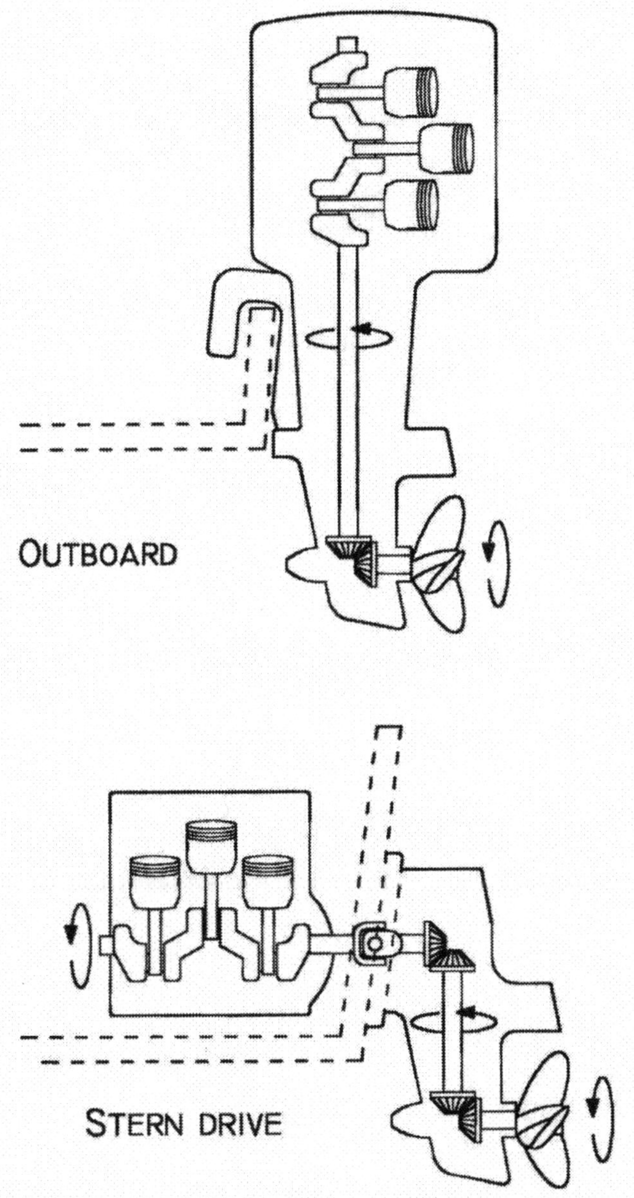

Figure 7

Gear paths of outboard and stern-drive systems

Another benefit made possible by a geared propeller shaft is the increase in efficiency that can be realized through the use of dual, counter-rotating propellers While the propellers appear to be mounted on a single shaft, they actually rotate on separate, concentric shafts – a shaft-within-a-shaft arrangement – that is not practical in inboard systems The added complexity and cost of such a system is offset by its ability to deliver more power to the water than a single propeller arrangement

Either system, outboard motor or stern-drive, provides overall manageability far superior to that of a single-screw inboard at a cost far less than a twin engine arrangement.

Chapter 6
SLOW-SPEED MANEUVERING TWIN-SCREW BOATS

Other than the dependability of having two engines, the most prominent feature of twin-screw boats is the maneuverability that comes from being able to control the output of their engines separately. Ironically, that feature can be a problem at cruising speeds where it is desirable to have both engines running at exactly the same speed. Engine synchronizers are regularly used to overcome the problem and the newer, electronic engine-control systems can do it automatically. The standard, inboard twin-screw system is widely accepted as the most maneuverable layout for use in medium- to-larger size vessels The underlying reason for its superior performance is that it provides more accurate control over the bow than any other propulsion system Twin stern drives may have a slight edge in maneuverability – especially at the stern - because of their ability to direct their thrust, but their power-handling limitation restricts their use on larger vessels.

Two levels of twin-screw maneuverability are shown in figures 8 and 9. Panel A in Figure 8 shows power being applied by the starboard engine only – the port engine is not in gear – which causes the boat to steer to port, pivoting around a theoretical point somewhat off its port side. The resulting course of the boat is shown in Panel B. Keep in mind, the boat will move in the direction opposite the propeller thrust.

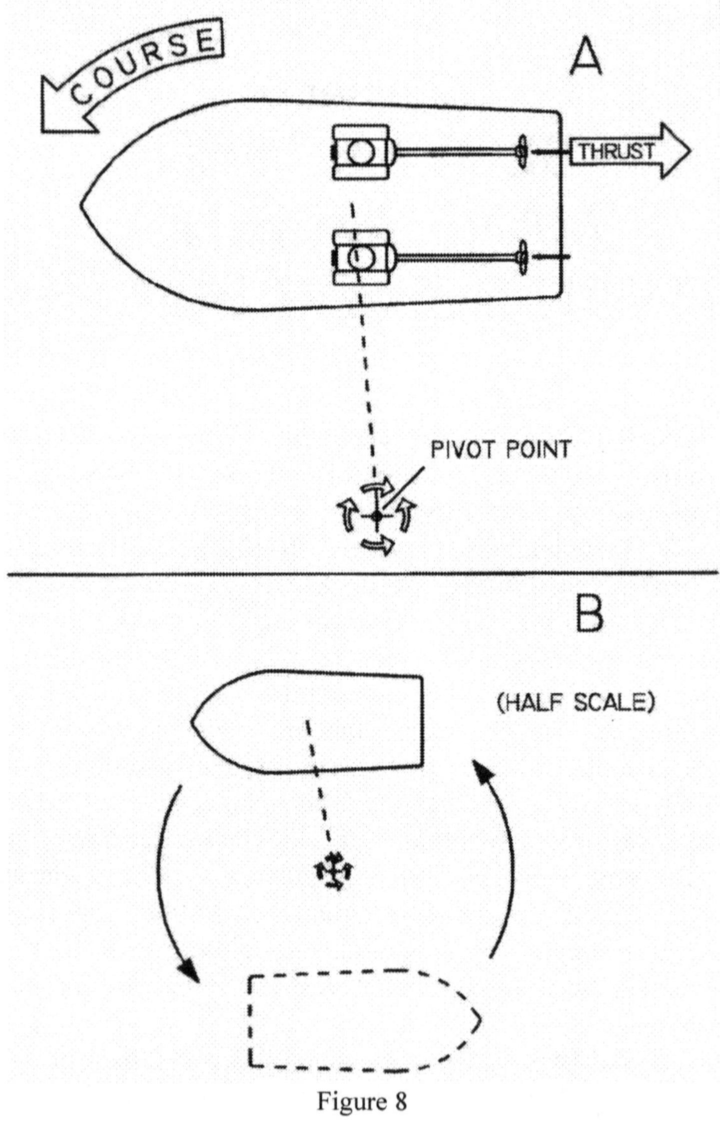

Figure 8

Turning using the thrust of a single engine

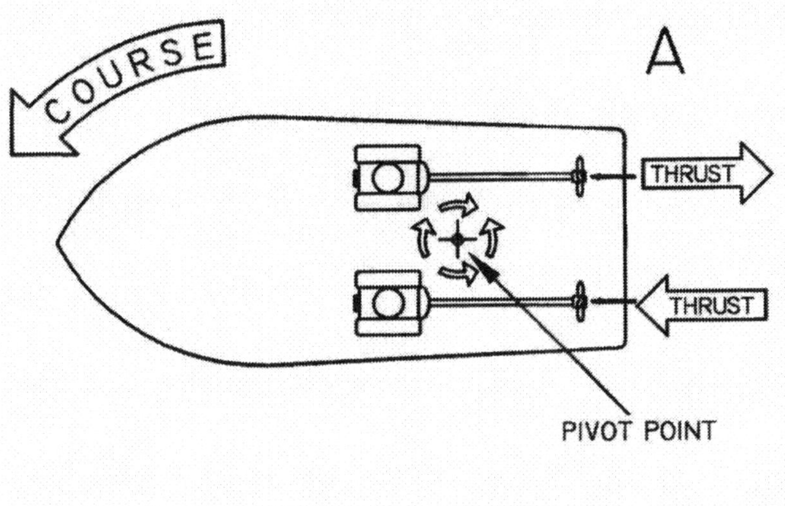

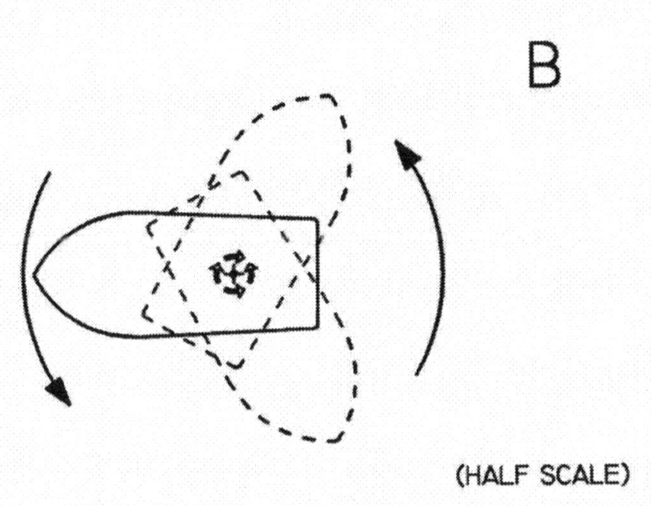

Figure 9

Turning using the opposing thrust of two engines

Figure 9 shows the same boat with power being applied in different directions simultaneously – the starboard engine in forward gear and the port engine in reverse. In this case, the theoretical pivot point is within the outline of the boat, resulting in a drastically decreased turning radius, as shown in Panel B. The boat is able to turn 360 degrees in its own length.

The turning radii and pivot points shown in these illustrations are for comparative purposes only. Actual turning radii and pivot points are determined by many variables and will be different for every boat.

The resulting control is so precise that most skippers do not use rudder steering at all during low speed maneuvers They set the engines' speed at idle and control the position of the boat by alternately using forward, reverse or neutral transmission gears. The rudders are used only at higher speeds. Even though the system significantly reduces the need for a bow thruster, some builders and owners take a belt-and-suspenders approach and include one for the slight edge in maneuverability it adds.

The advantage in maneuverability that is provided by a twin-screw system is dependent on the distance between the two propellers. The distance is important because the two propellers are actually operating at a mechanical disadvantage when trying to move the bow, since the distance to the bow is greater than their separation. In the case of a larger boat, where the propellers may be ten feet apart, they have far more mechanical advantage in moving the bow from side-to-side than they would have if they were placed more closely together. If they were installed on a 40-foot boat, for example, they would operate at a 1:4 disadvantage.

In the opposite situation, where two outboard motors are mounted side-by-side on small boat, they are less likely to be used to maneuver as shown in Figure 9, because their proximity to each other makes their mechanical advantage less effective for such a maneuver. If they were 4 feet apart on a 30-foot boat, they would operate at a 1:7.5 disadvantage. These ratios are generalizations, but are useful for illustration.

Chapter 7
DOCKING

When a friend and I were shopping for my first boat, we came across a good-looking 24-foot Rampage on a trailer.

"Here's a boat that's spent its entire life on a mooring or a trailer," my friend declared after inspecting it closely.

"How can you tell?" I asked.

"No dock dings. No scratches. The topsides are perfect. Looks like its never been near a dock," he replied. He was right, and his comments have stayed with me for years in the form of a healthy respect for the consequences of docking ineptly.

Most boat owners will admit to an uneasy feeling when approaching a dock. It is, after all, a prime opportunity to come in contact with a relatively immovable object, with a real chance of causing damage to the boat. The condition of many docks - exposed hardware and sharp, unforgiving edges - just adds to the anxiety. All of the outside influences that affect maneuverability seem to be magnified when you are faced with a solid barrier and the restricted room resulting from the presence of other boats or nearby hazards. It doesn't help that there is often an audience of onlookers eager to be entertained by your performance.

Unfortunately, there are few hard and fast rules for docking because the conditions are always changing. It is different every time. You can stack the deck in your favor, however, by making sure you are prepared with a plan and the boat has the right equipment.

Preparing to dock

Your preparation should begin with an assessment of the conditions in the immediate area Check your telltale or nearby flags to gauge the wind Look at moored boats or objects floating on the water to check the current Think about how the conditions you see will affect the course you will take and your ability to control the boat If the wind is blowing toward the dock, for example, you will want to steer a course further away from the dock and allow the wind to move you in If the wind or current is on your stern, you will want to go in more slowly and plan to shift into reverse earlier to halt your forward progress The ability to make such decisions may become second-nature with experience, but making them up-front and discussing the plan with your crew or passengers will always be the best way to avoid embarrassment or worse Take your time - maybe even pass by the dock once or twice to go through the maneuver mentally before you head in

The immediate preparation of the boat for docking consists of stowing loose gear, deploying your fenders, attaching fore and aft dock lines and making sure they are positioned for easy access, but not lying on the deck or walkways where you could trip over them

The real preparation of your boat should have started before you launched it Many of the conditions that contribute to safe and successful docking revolve around how well your boat is equipped and the condition of your gear The absence of midships cleats on many pleasure boats is a common problem because manufacturers choose to omit them to save a buck or two. If your boat doesn't have them, you should add them They are relatively easy to install and provide a tie point for fenders and spring lines, whose importance we will discuss in following chapters.

It is a rare boat that has a sufficient number of tie points for fenders. The ones that do, seem to have them placed everywhere but where you need them One of the most important places for a fender is at the point where the hull side begins to curve in to become the bow. This is the first part of the boat that could make contact during a docking approach and should be protected by a fender. If your boat has no tie point there - a cleat or rail stanchion - install one.

Equipping the boat with appropriate dock lines is important too. There are many types and sizes of cordage (they are *ropes* on shore and *lines* on board, but the general term is *cordage*) and it is important to match both to the boat and their use. Nylon is the best material for dock lines because it protects boats and cleats by stretching to absorb shock. Braided line is stronger and easier to handle. Three-strand twisted line stretches more and costs less. For boats up to 25 feet long, 3/8" diameter line of either type is adequate. For larger boats or severe conditions, ½" line is better, but make sure your cleats are sized to accept it before you buy. Catalogs published by Boat U.S., West Marine and other outlets have instructional sections that can be invaluable in helping you make the correct choice of lines for every situation.

For a small-to-medium sized boat, you should have at least two dock lines that are about twice as long as your boat is wide, and a spring line that is as least as long as your boat. Many boaters prefer a compliment of five lines, adding a pair of slightly longer dock lines that can be used when dock cleats are not close. The longer lines can also be used as individual spring lines when the need arises and can be thrown further in difficult situations. A complete set of five, with eyes already spliced in can be bought for as little as seventy dollars - inexpensive insurance when you consider the cost of the boat. If your boat spends a lot of time at a particular dock, you can adjust line lengths to suit specific conditions, but don't be fooled into thinking that longer is better. Excess length just makes lines more difficult to handle and stow. Lines should be kept in good condition, free of cuts, kinks and knots and be replaced as soon as they begin to fray.

Remember to rig your lines and fenders well in advance of docking. There are few things more distracting than a last-minute rush to get lines secured and a distraction is the last thing you need during a docking maneuver.

Docking under various conditions

There are two instructions that apply to all docking maneuvers, approach slowly - but under power - and make sure your crew or passengers know what you are going to do and what you expect of them. Whether they are part of the plan or you just want them to stand clear, tell them ahead of time to avoid confusion.

Approaching the dock slowly enhances your ability to abort the maneuver if something goes wrong. Approaching under power gives you the most positive control because you are creating directional thrust (in the case of an outdrive or outboard), or pushing water past the rudder of an inboard. If you coast toward the dock, it requires you to throttle back or even take the boat out of gear, greatly reducing your control. A good way to accommodate both needs - slow speed and maintaining power - is to bring the boat to a stop just before making the final turn into the dock. Then put it back in gear to finish the approach - slowly, under power and in control. If you need to approach even more slowly than the idling engine will allow, shift the transmission out of gear briefly to match your speed to the conditions, but remember that you need power to maintain control.

Docking Abeam

Docking abeam is the marine equivalent of parallel parking. When you are lucky enough to face ideal conditions there will be an unobstructed dock, no wind and no current, so your approach and docking maneuver can be something like that shown in Figure 10. Make the initial approach (1) at an angle to the dock with the rudder in the neutral position.

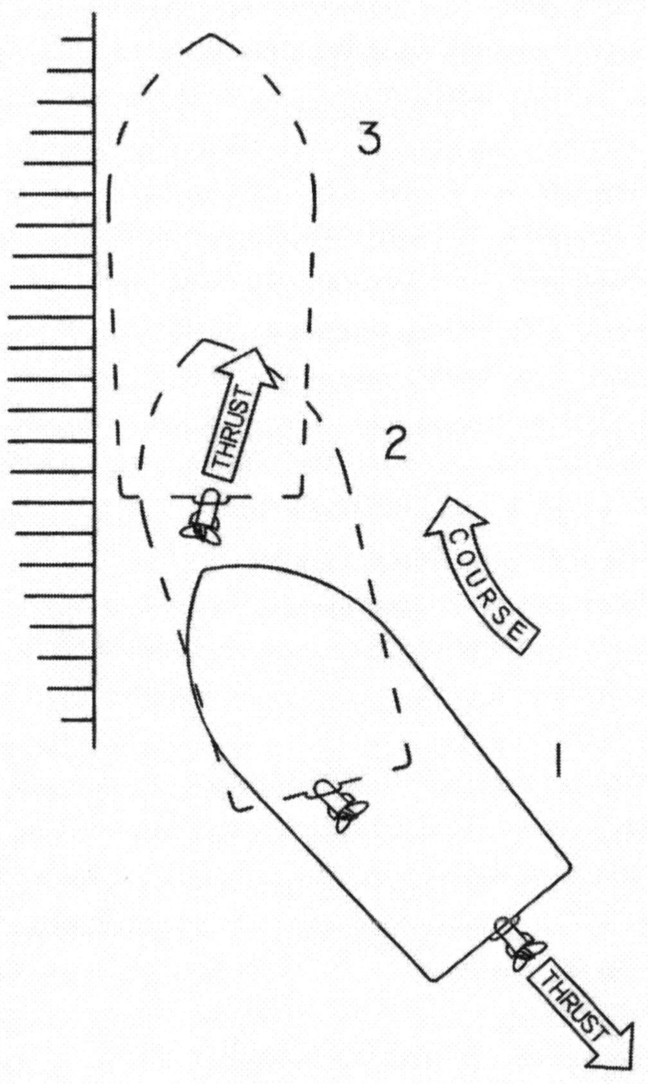

Figure 10

Docking abeam under normal conditions

(The term *rudder* is used as a description of *steering position* regardless of whether the action involves a rudder, an outdrive or an outboard.) As the boat nears the dock (2), turn the rudder to starboard to initiate the turn. As the stern swings around so the boat is parallel with the dock (3), bring the rudder back to a neutral position and reverse the thrust to halt forward progress. If the stern doesn't tuck in completely, turn the rudder to port while applying power in reverse. In the case of an inboard where propwalk occurs in the wrong direction for the occasion, turn the rudder completely to starboard and apply a short burst of forward power to push the stern over.

Docking Abeam in a Beam Wind

Docking abeam in the presence of either wind or current, requires some forethought to determine whether you will have to fight the external influences or use them to your advantage. There are several scenarios to consider.

If the wind direction is at a right angle to the dock and blowing toward it, docking may be as simple as stopping the boat in a position off the dock and allowing the wind to push you gently into place. When the wind is coming from the opposite direction, the docking procedure will be as shown in Figure 10, except you will have to approach the dock more forcefully to overcome the wind resistance. Also, you will have a shorter period of time to make your dock lines fast before the wind blows the boat back off the dock This is a situation where quick actions are required, so the time you took to prepare lines and instruct the crew will pay off in the form of a quick and efficient tie-up.

Docking Abeam with Wind or Current on the Bow

Any time a strong wind or current is encountered, you should head *into* it when docking if you have a choice This is a situation where you can use the outside influences to your advantage, since you may actually gain more control by heading into an opposing force like wind or current

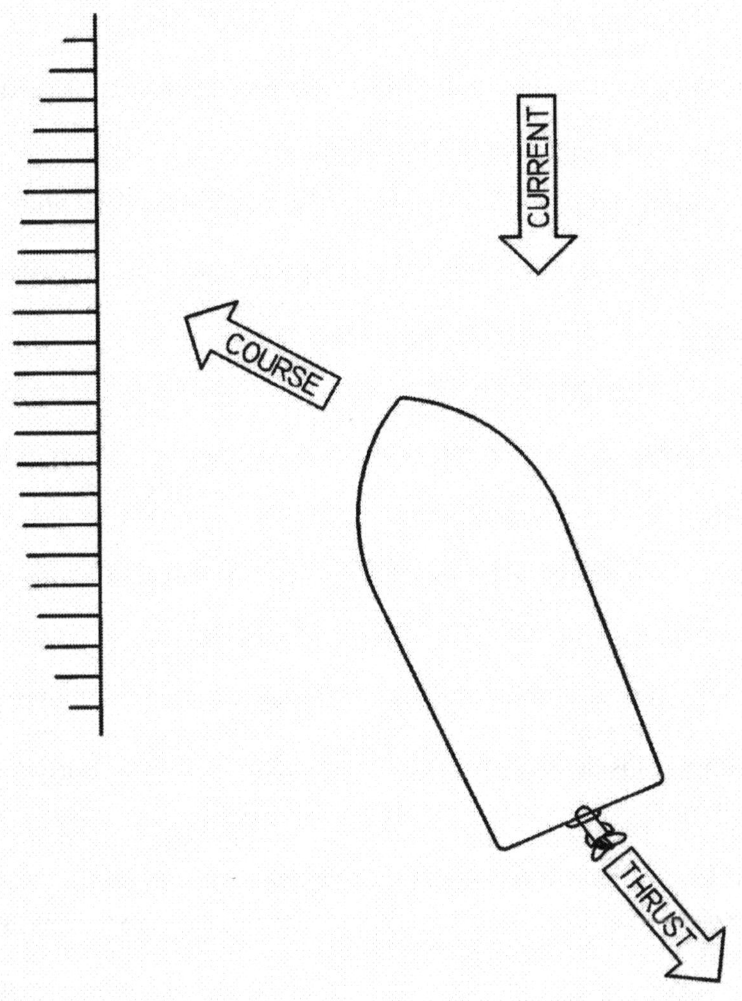

Figure 11

Docking with wind or current on the bow

You will notice two effects. More power will be required to maintain headway speed and you will have to compensate for the opposing force by keeping the bow pointed more toward it as you head for the dock. Unlike the straight-line approach shown in Figure 10, you will end up "crabbing" across to the dock. This is a situation where your bow is pointed midway between your intended course and the direction from which the wind or current is coming Looking closely at Figure 11, you will see that the rudder is turned slightly to starboard to maintain bow position, resulting in a situation where both the rudder and the keel are at an angle to the intended course.

This is a maneuver that requires a delicate balance between rudder position and power being applied to maintain the proper course. Too little power or not enough starboard rudder will cause the boat to lose forward speed and veer to port. Too much power or starboard rudder will cause it to move too far to starboard. It is a maneuver that requires practice, but becomes second-nature very quickly.

Docking Abeam with Wind or Current on the Stern

This is a situation that even causes anxiety among the pros, but it is not always avoidable. (Some river marinas, for example, insist that all boats dock with their bow upriver to reduce the strain on their dock systems.) The root of the difficulty is lack of control. The wind or current abaft increases the boat's speed in a situation where excess speed is not desirable. The instinctive reaction is to throttle back to reduce speed, but this results in a nearly complete loss of control and the only way to regain control is to speed up. It is a prime example of a Catch-22 situation.

Figure 12 illustrates the danger inherent in trying to head into a dock with the force of strong wind or current behind you. If your forward speed is less than the speed of the wind or current, it will invariably push the stern away from the dock and forward, putting the boat in an awkward and potentially dangerous position from which it is difficult to recover. Trying to pull the stern back in by using reverse thrust will simply result in the bow swinging away from the dock.

An experienced skipper who knows the boat very well may take a *kamikaze* approach - head in uncomfortably fast to ensure a high level of control and then apply a substantial burst of reverse thrust just in time to halt the boat's forward motion at the dock. It is maneuver that really impresses an audience when it is successful (or entertains them when it is not), but has very little room for error, especially in tight quarters, and is definitely not for the novice or the faint-of-heart.

A more comfortable, though less conventional approach is to back into the berth. By backing into the wind or current, you have the freedom to apply more power for control purposes while not unduly increasing your speed, so the boat can be steered into place. As shown in Figure 13, the wind or current will actually assist you by pushing the bow into the dock as you back up, but be sure to keep an eye on it, especially if there is another boat at the dock in front of your slot. Remember that your control over the bow while backing up is tenuous at best, leaving it free to be pushed around by external forces.

Backing in is an option available to all except some single-screw inboards, which may have trouble with the maneuver because of a lack of control in reverse. Those fitted with a bow thruster, however, have a better chance since the thruster can be used to move the bow from side-to-side, steering the boat as it backs up. It takes practice, but it can be done.

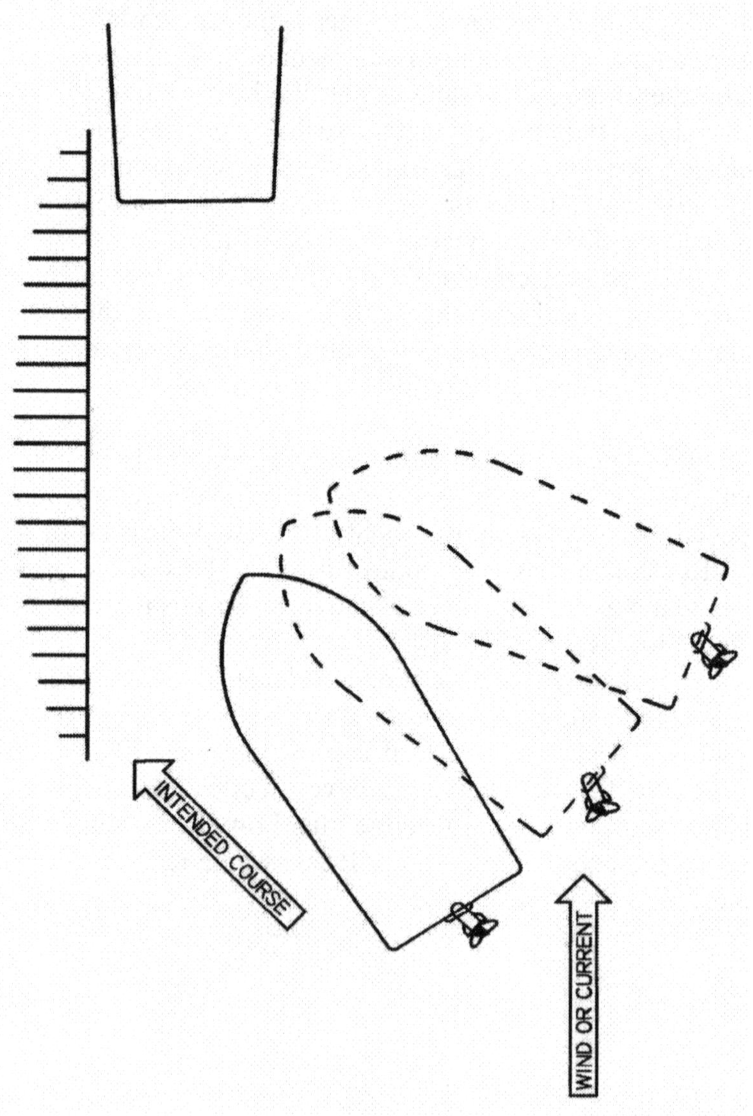

Figure 12

The unintended results of trying to dock with wind or current astern

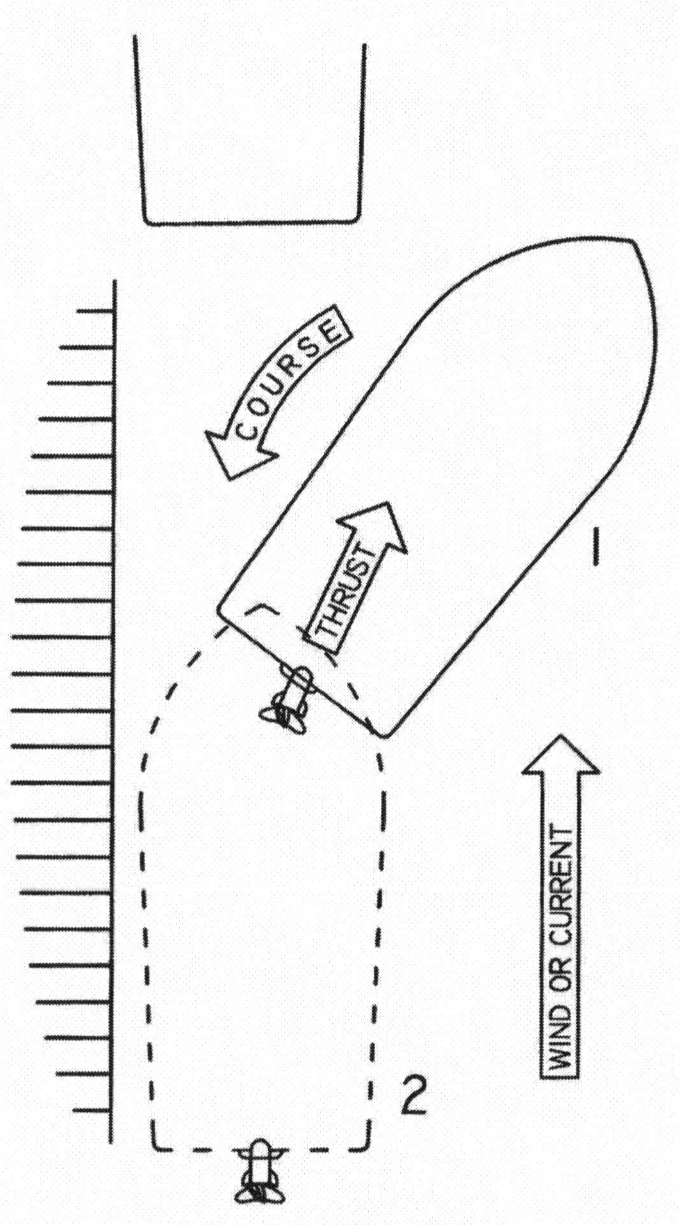

Figure 13

Docking by backing into a wind or current

Docking in Limited Space

One of the most daunting tasks a skipper can face is docking in a limited space. It would be nice if we were always faced with ideal conditions - an empty dock, no wind and no current - but more often than not there will be other boats at the dock. Restricted maneuvering space necessitates very precise control during docking maneuvers, a situation that favors twin-screw boats and those equipped with bow thrusters. The rest - a majority - will have to rely on patience, good judgement and the timely use of docking aids such as active spring lines. It can be a situation that makes a willing dock hand look like a white knight.

It is also a situation that demands a thorough evaluation of available options. Unless the space is severely restricted, a careful approach using one of the methods described earlier may be all that is needed. If you are boating alone and there is no one on the dock to assist you, it may be the only option. If there is someone on the dock to assist you, they can catch a thrown line and use it to warp you into place. If conditions do not allow that, the use of an active spring line may be the next best alternative.

An *active* spring line (*passive* ones are discussed in Chapter 8) is a line that is made fast to a point on the boat and to the dock to assist in maneuvering the boat. Properly placed, it limits the forward (or rearward) motion of the boat and provides a pair of pivot points around which the boat can be rotated to bring it into the desired position at the dock. To use the spring-line technique, make a line fast to a midships or forward cleat and throw the bitter end to the dockhand. Instruct him to bend it around an after cleat as shown in Figure 14. He should not secure it, but just take a single turn around the cleat - enough to give him a purchase that will allow him to keep the boat from moving too far forward, yet allow him to adjust its length if required.

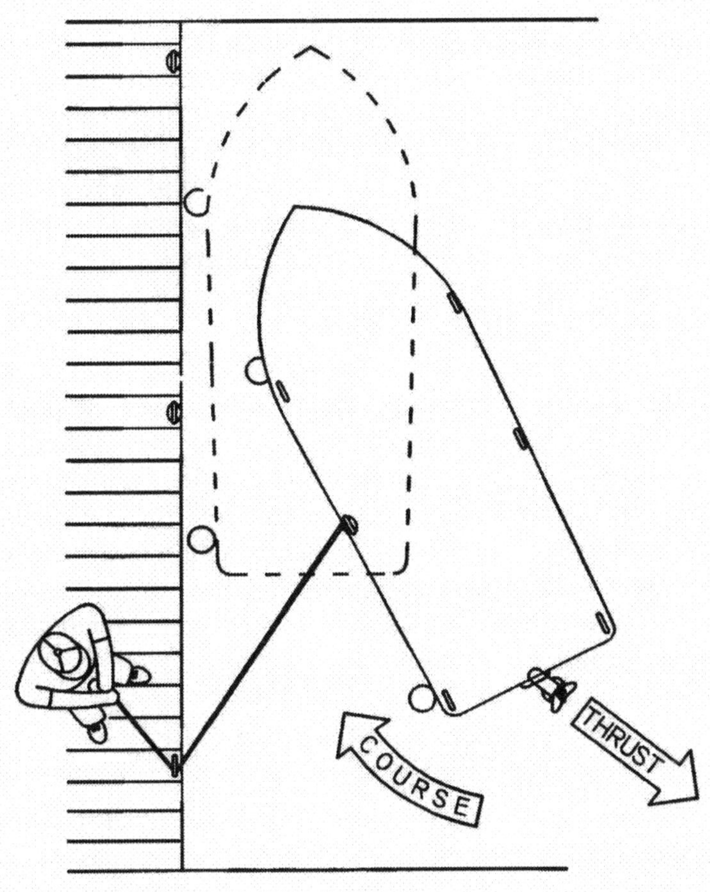

Figure 14

Using an active spring line to dock in a tight berth

Turn the rudder fully to starboard and apply just enough thrust to move the boat forward, but because it is tethered by the spring line, the boat will also rotate around the pivot point at the midships cleat. As the stern begins to tuck in, the boat and the spring line will also rotate around the pivot point at the dock cleat, bringing the stern close enough to the dock to throw a stern line ashore. Once the bow and stern dock lines are secured, rig the *passive* spring lines (See

Chapter 8) to control fore-and-aft motion while the boat is tied up. Again, the most important function of the *active* spring line is to allow power to be used to maneuver the boat, while preventing the boat from hitting obstructions, either fore or aft

The spring-line technique can also be used when backing a boat into place, but its usefulness will be restricted to limiting the travel of the boat unless it is feasible to secure the line to the outboard side of the boat. Otherwise, the bow will move away from the dock if reverse thrust is continued after the line has become taut.

In any situation where spring lines are used in docking, it is important to protect the boat with fenders at potential contact points fore and aft. These maneuvers should be practiced before a need arises to sort out the peculiarities and behavior of the boat under these conditions. The placement of cleats, for example, may be such that using a forward cleat is a better choice than the midships cleat. You must know that before you are forced to use the maneuver to avoid dinging someone's million-dollar yacht.

Drive-in or Back-in Slips

Many large marinas have drive-in and back-in slips on opposite sides of long fairways. In many ways, it is easier to get in and out of these slips than it is to dock abeam, but there are, of course, exceptions. Under normal conditions, the main difference is that getting into a drive-in slip will be easier if you stop and get lined up first, rather than trying to make it into the slip in one sweeping turn. In the case of a back-in slip, you must come to a stop to change direction anyway, so the maneuver comes naturally. If there is wind on your stern as you proceed down the fairway, you may want to go beyond your slip and turn around so you can make the turn to get lined up with the wind on your bow. Other than that, the same over-all rule - go in slowly and under power - applies.

All of the effects of external conditions - wind and current - that have been mentioned in the earlier discussions of docking abeam apply to docking in a fairway slip as well One exceptional situation that may be encountered (especially if you dock on a river), is backing into a slip with a strong wind or current on your bow. In such an instance, getting the boat lined up in front of the slip is even more important, but instead of putting the boat in reverse to back in, you should leave it in forward gear and adjust the throttle to a setting where the speed of the boat matches the speed of the wind or current At that point the boat will be stationary in the water, but can still be moved from side-to-side by steering with the rudder. This allows you to maintain your alignment with the slip as you back off the throttle just enough to allow the boat to move aft toward the slip. As with any maneuver in reverse, keep an eye on the bow as you back up, but be especially vigilant because the wind or current can displace it very quickly in a situation such as this. When the boat is in position in the slip, a slight increase in throttle - still in forward gear - will bring it to a stop while you make a bow line fast.

Docking Single-handed

Many people find the peace and solitude of boating alone to be one of life's great pleasures - until it is time to dock, that is. It can be a challenge for a novice, but one that abates with time and experience.

Preparation can make the task much easier. Setting out fenders and leading the bow and stern dock lines back to a position on the boat where you can access them should be part of the routine. Coil the bitter ends of the lines to insure they will not be underfoot. You should be able to use the procedures discussed earlier to get the boat into position at the dock and, under normal conditions, be able to debark with dock line in hand to secure the boat. In the presence of wind or current, however, it may make sense to set up a temporary dock line that will allow you to tether the boat to the dock without having to debark.

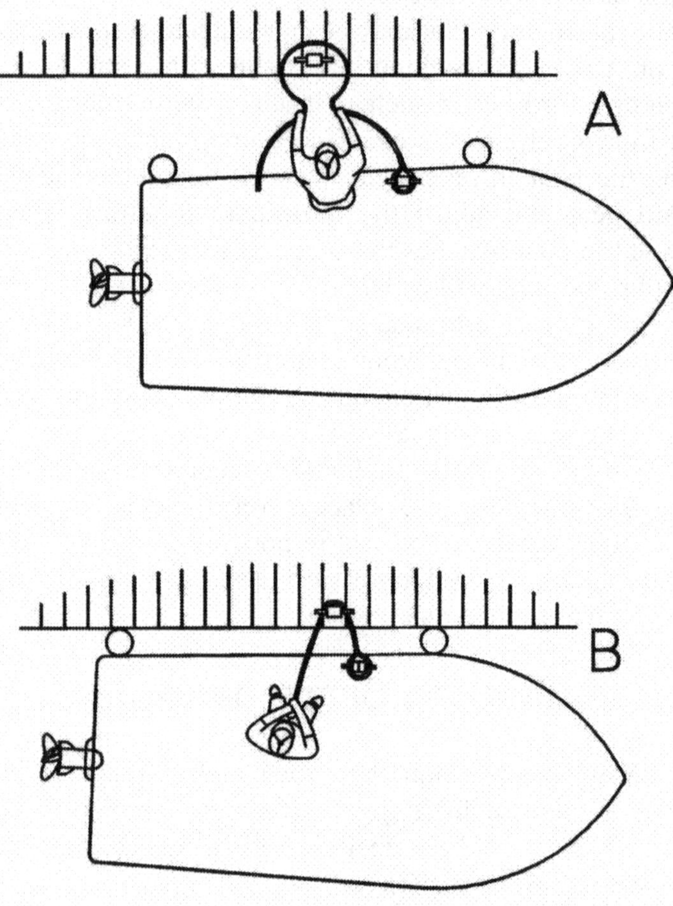

Figure 15

Rigging a temporary dockline

To set up a temporary dock line, make one end of a line fast to a midships cleat, then run it outside any railings or obstructions and lead it back to a position where you can access it, leaving a generous loop in the line before you coil the bitter end. Your other lines should be prepared as discussed above. Identify the position of a cleat on the dock and maneuver the boat to the dock so that the cleat is within reach from your access point on the boat Leave the helm long enough to quickly place the loop of your temporary dock line around the cleat as shown in Panel A of Figure 15, then pull in the bitter end to draw the boat as close to the dock as possible (Panel B). Tie the bitter end to any nearby point on the boat, a cleat, a rail stanchion or even a seat post to keep the boat in place while you make more permanent arrangements

Chapter 8
SECURING THE BOAT

There are those who would argue that tying a boat to a dock is not rocket science. They deem it a success if they tie up, go off to do their thing and come back and the boat is still there. Their logic is irrefutable, but there is more to it than looping a line on a cleat.

Securing the boat is the most important consideration, but avoiding damage to your boat and others around you is important too. The overall goal is to secure the boat so you control what the hull comes in contact with - ideally, only its fenders. Contact with anything else can result in damage. And, there is the harder-to-define goal of keeping your pride intact by making it look like you know what you are doing.

The basic complement of lines for docking consists of bow and stern dock lines and at least one passive spring line. Spring lines are used in two different ways *Active* spring lines are used to provide a pivot point to maneuver a boat in a tight spot or away from a dock against wind or current. They are discussed in the two previous chapters and the next. *Passive* spring lines are used as part of the system that secures the boat to the dock. Many people get confused about spring lines because, like the sails on a clipper ship, their name varies according to their position. Remember passive spring lines have only one function - to control the fore and aft movement of your boat while the bow and stern dock lines keep the boat parallel and secured to the dock (or other boat when rafting).

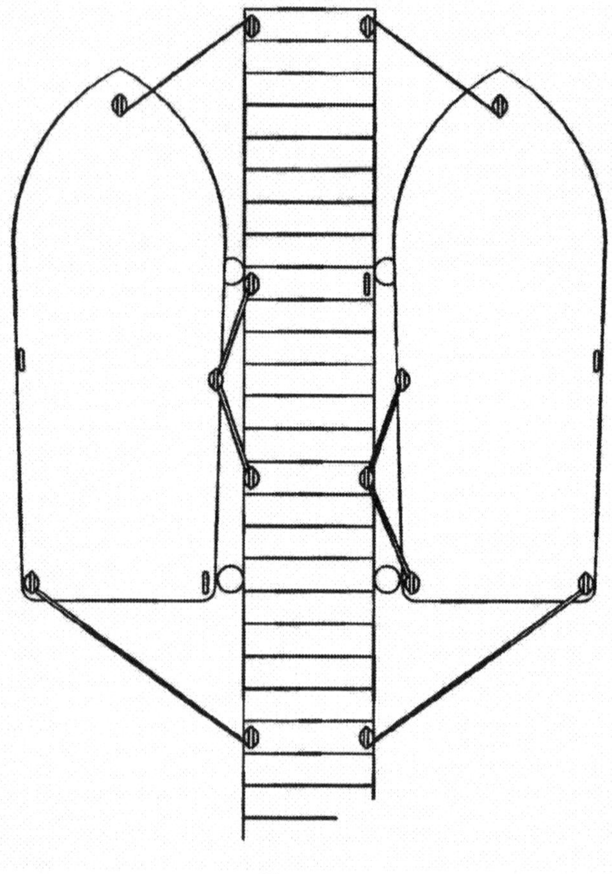

Figure 16

Two different spring line setups

Figure 16 shows tie-ups using two popular spring line arrangements. Both use traditional bow and stern lines and a single spring line secured to three points. Separate spring lines in other fore-and-aft configurations can be used as long as they control the movement of the boat in either direction The use of spring lines is especially important in areas that are affected by strong current or wind and, in fact, many marinas in such locations require them to be used for any tie-up.

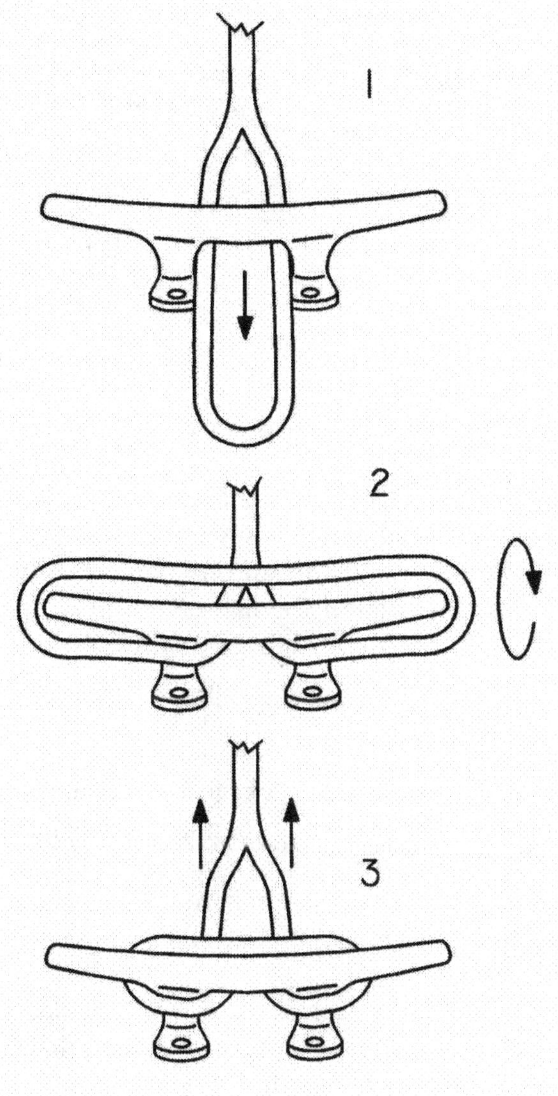

Figure 17

Securing the eye of a line to a cleat

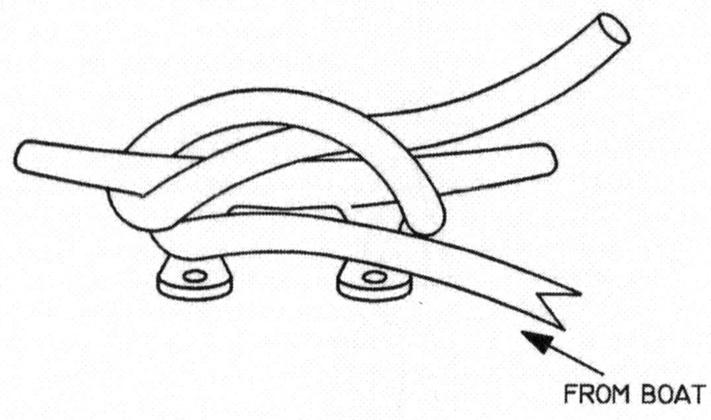

Figure 18

The bitter end of a line secured to a cleat

Most people buy ready-made dock lines that have had an eye spliced into one end. The eye makes it easy to secure the working end of the line to an on-board cleat as shown in Figure 17. The bitter end of the line is free to be made fast to the dock. If the fixture on the dock is a traditional cleat, the line should be bent once around it and secured with a half-hitch as shown in Figure 18. Any excess line can be wrapped around the cleat in figure-eight fashion, flemished on the dock or – if it is long enough - doubled back to the boat cleat. These measures mainly keep it from becoming a tripping hazard on the dock, but they also result in a neater, more professional look. In some cases, excess line can be used as a spring line by tying it back to a midships cleat. Such an arrangement is shown in Figure 19.

Another consideration in the use of bow and stern dock lines is the need for adequate distance between their tie points. The shock-absorbing qualities of a nylon line increase with its length. A very short dock line, from a stern cleat to an adjacent dock cleat, may not absorb the shock of wakes or rough weather, putting undue stress on the mounting of the cleat. A better solution is to run the line to the far side of the boat as shown in Figure 16, resulting in a longer, more forgiving line.

Finally, the boat should not be drawn up so tightly to the dock that the fenders are compressed by the tension The fenders will eventually be displaced by the pressure, leaving the boat to chafe on the dock The lines should be long enough so the boat can rest away from the dock and allow the fender to drop back in place after being compressed by a wave or wake.

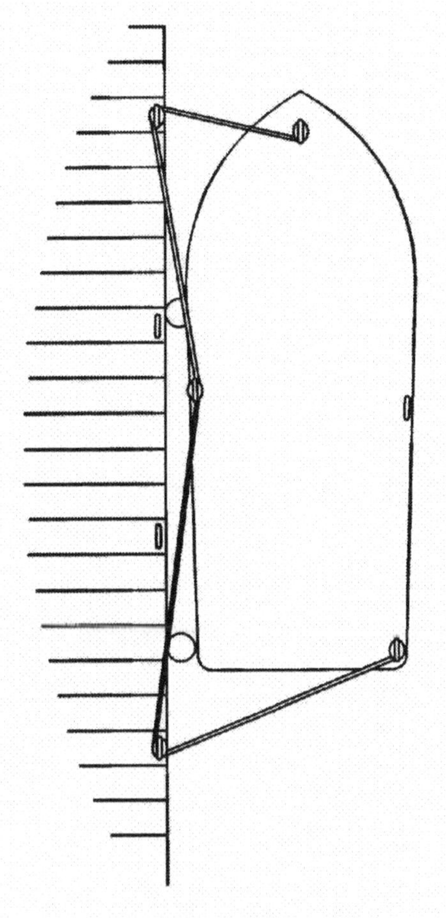

Figure 19

An alternate spring line setup

Chapter 9
DEPARTING THE DOCK

Departing the dock is usually more comfortable than an approach because of the feeling of moving away from the potential danger, but it still deserves your undivided attention. Before casting off, you should assess the surroundings and conditions and know how they will affect you. Make sure your rudder is properly positioned for the course you intend to take upon departure. Check for traffic in the waterway and look for other boats that may be preparing to depart. Look at telltales or flags around you to check the wind direction and be alert to the effects of current in the area. Any one of them can foil your best efforts if you are unprepared for their effects.

In the absence of wind or current, you should be able to simply untie your lines and push far enough off the dock to provide some maneuvering room during departure. Remember, your stern will swing toward the dock as you make the turn to leave in forward gear. Under less serene conditions, you can rig a temporary dock line (as described in Chapter 7) to hold the boat in place while you or a crewmember untie the dock lines. When you are ready to depart, release the bitter end and pull the temporary line back on board by its working end, being careful to keep it from fouling your prop.

Departing when a beam wind is pushing the boat into the dock is a more challenging situation. Figure 20 depicts a tried-and-true solution that employs an active spring line to allow you to back out of the berth. Rig a spring line from a forward point on the boat, aft to a dock cleat If there is no one on the dock to assist you, rig it in the same manner as a temporary dock line so a crew member can retrieve it at the appropriate time. Note the additional fender placed to protect the topsides forward.

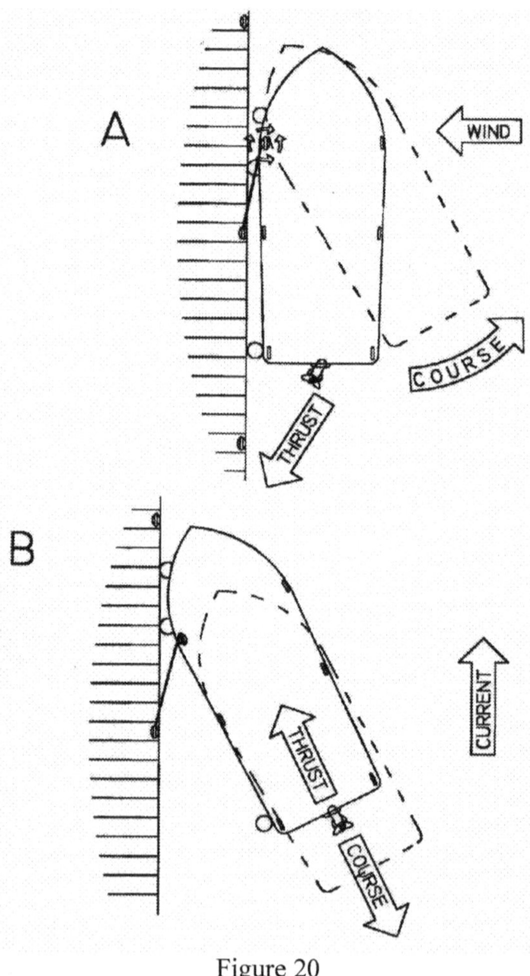

Figure 20

Using an active spring line to back away from the dock in a beam wind

Turn the rudder hard to port and engage forward gear at idle speed or under just enough power to overcome the effects of the wind. The boat will pivot on the forward tie point and swing its stern away from the dock as shown in Panel A of Figure 20. At the point where the boat is clear of any obstructions, turn the rudder back to center, engage reverse gear and cast off the spring line as you back away from the dock. This maneuver is also a good one to use with a current on your stern or when departing from a restricted space.

Figure 21 shows the details of using the same type of procedure to depart in forward, rather than in reverse. Note that this procedure may not be the best one for a boat with a swim platform or other structure protruding from the transom, as it relies on an aft corner of the boat coming in solid contact with the dock - cushioned by a fender. Rig an active spring line from an aft cleat to a forward dock cleat. Again, rig it as a temporary line if there is no helper ashore. Engage reverse gear to cause the boat to pivot around the aft cleat and swing the bow out to starboard (Panel A). Then engage forward gear and head away from the dock, pausing long enough to retrieve the spring line. Since the spring line will be in the water behind you, take great care to keep it from fouling the prop.

The methods shown in Figures 20 & 21 are relatively straightforward, but both deserve some practice in a non-threatening situation before you need to use them. In any case, the success of an operation involving the use of an active spring line depends on good communication between the skipper and the crewmember handling the spring line. If the spring line is released prematurely, the pivot point on which you are depending disappears along with your control of the situation. If it is not released on time, it can impede your progress or put you in a dangerous position. Make sure your crewmember understands his or her role, your expectations and the signals you will use to communicate.

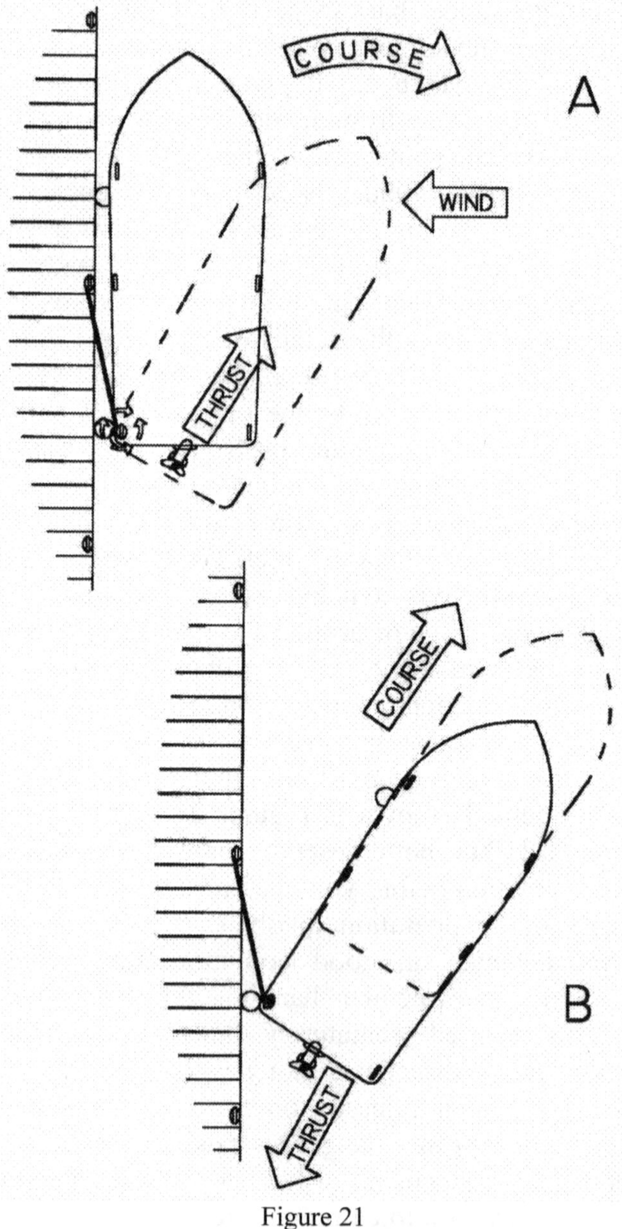

Figure 21

Using an active spring line to depart from the dock in a beam wind

If you find you use active spring lines on a regular basis, it will pay you to buy one made out of polypropylene, which floats. It will not have the comfort and ease of handling that nylon does and should not be used as a full-time dock line, but it will be less likely to end up in your prop when used as an active spring line.

NOTE: In any situation where active spring lines are employed to maneuver a boat, a great deal of tension will be applied to the spring line. It is important to insure that both ends are secured in a manner to accept the load and crew members are instructed to stand clear during operations. The same care should be taken in employing fenders – both in number and location - to protect the topsides of the boat, as considerable pressure may be applied to them when pivoting against the dock.

Chapter 10
UNDER WAY

Under way describes all movement between the time you leave the dock and arrive at your destination, without regard to how fast you travel or how far you go. Under way can mean a trip across a pond that requires little more than common sense and a sense of direction. Or it can mean an off-shore cruise that taxes your endurance and takes advantage of everything you've learned through years of experience, but that is a level of seamanship far beyond what we could teach here.

Boat handling is a part of seamanship, but the term usually conveys a sense of activities that take place at slower speeds and in closer proximity to shore facilities and other craft. Neither of those conditions should be taken as an excuse to be less vigilant or an indication that less skill is required of the skipper.

The proximity to other boats, for example, means that your ability to control yours is critical. Boats do not turn and stop on the proverbial dime, so anticipation is a skill essential to boat handling. In boating, as in a chess game, the ability to react is often not enough. You have to continually evaluate the overall situation and know how you will deal with the possibilities as they crop up. Anticipation is important when you enter a channel, inlet or some area where your ability to maneuver will be restricted. This is especially true if your boat has high windage or single screw propulsion that will impact handling or limit your ability to react. If you allow wind or current to drive you too close to shore or other obstacles, you may not have sufficient room to maneuver away. Anticipating their effect will help you recognize the need to stay on the upwind or upcurrent side of the inlet in relative safety.

Practice to determine the turning and stopping characteristics of your boat. You should know exactly what your boat will do when a shot of power in reverse is required to bring it to a quick stop. Applying excess power in reverse will cause some outboards and outdrives to tilt up and out of the water, resulting in a loss of thrust , which in this case means a loss of stopping power. You should be familiar with those types of limitations before you encounter an emergency.

One exercise that may accelerate your learning process is to make a list of the maneuvers or activities that give you the greatest problems or cause the most discomfort. Rig some extra fenders for protection, then find a relatively remote location - an un-used dock or a float in a mooring field - where you can practice those maneuvers without worrying about an audience or being embarrassed by an occasional miss. You can squeeze a full season of experience into just a few hours of practice, significantly add to your abilities and make a real difference in your comfort level.

Boats of all sizes should be loaded evenly, but the smaller the boat, the more important it becomes. A small boat that is either overloaded, or has all of its passengers concentrated in the bow, will not only lose much of its maneuverability, but is in real danger of being swamped by an unexpected wave or wake. The danger is just as great when the load is concentrated aft or on one side. You may be able to use trim tabs (see Chapter 11) to compensate for the imbalance in some cases, but redistributing the load is a much safer solution.

Navigating the wakes of other boats, especially ones that are larger than yours, can be a source of aggravation and danger. You should cross the wake of a boat that has overtaken you at as great an angle as possible to prevent your boat from rolling from side-to-side excessively. Remember to check aft for following traffic before making your turn. When you attempt to cross the wake of a boat you are overtaking, do it at a point as far aft of the other boat as possible and at a right angle to the wake. Make sure your passengers are ready for a rough ride and be prepared to apply considerably more power to overcome the resistance as you push through the turbulence of the wake. Wakes – especially those of large boats – contain a tremendous amount of kinetic energy that can be difficult to overcome.

There are no lanes, median strips or stoplights on the water, so safe and successful navigation – especially in restricted or crowded waterways - depends on boats being operated in an orderly, predictable manner. There are well-defined and extensive rules for operating offshore* and on inland waterways** and all boaters who operate there should be familiar with their basic requirements, but more often than not, *orderly* and *predictable* conditions are the result of common courtesy.

Courtesy covers a wide range of situations, including giving way to other craft when required, being responsible for your wake, keeping to the side of a restricted channel and even using the proper VHF channels for communication. (See Appendix B, *The* Very *Unofficial Rules of the Road.*)

It has been my observation that sailors are generally more courteous and rules-oriented than powerboaters. (I can say that because I am a dedicated stink-potter.) Perhaps the extended apprenticeship that most sailors go through – there is a lot to learn to become an able sailor – imbues a sense of courtesy and adherence to the rules. On the other hand, nearly anyone can turn the ignition key and motor off in a power boat without the least training or exposure to the rules of the road in most states. With more than thirteen million pleasure boats in use in the US at this writing, that is probably a situation that will not and should not be allowed to exist much longer.

* *International Regulations for Preventing Collisions at Sea*, called COLREGS by the Coast Guard and also known as The Rules of the Road.

** *Inland Rules*, which regulate activities in harbors

and navigable inland lakes, rivers and waterways.

Chapter 11
HANDLING A SMALL BOAT IN HEAVY SEAS

Every boater who ventures into rough water has a responsibility to insure that he and his boat are prepared to handle it. Of course, the most effective way of avoiding danger is to stay in port when conditions are unfavorable. Unfortunately, even the most prudent boater can get caught in a sudden weather change or wind shift and have to navigate heavy seas to get back into port, so it makes sense to be prepared. The first thing to do when you are confronted with the possibility of heavy seas is to prepare your boat.

Batten down. Close and latch ports, hatches and companionway doors to keep water from flowing below decks If your boat has any hawse pipes that lead to anchor lockers or other enclosed spaces, stuff rags into them to keep water from building up in them.

Pump the bilge dry. Excess water in the bilge is unstable ballast that can affect handling and reduce buoyancy.

Check the scuppers. Remove any debris that could prevent the free passage of water through the scuppers and stow any loose material that could be swept into them Any water you may take on needs to drain off as quickly as possible.

Distribute weight. Imbalances that were just inconvenient under normal conditions can be downright dangerous in heavy seas. An overloaded bow may lack the buoyancy to rise over a wave. A heavy stern can lead to being "pooped" - water coming in over the transom. Direct passengers to specific spots and tell them to stay put.

Secure loose gear. Heavy objects, such as coolers or dive gear should be tied down or stowed in compartments to keep them from moving around in the cockpit.

Use PFDs. Everyone on board, including the skipper, should don their PFDs and insure they are properly cinched up. Make sure throwable PFDs or flotation cushions are handy and everyone knows about them.

Know where you are. Take location readings on a regular basis if you have GPS or LORAN, or note the bearings of landmarks and aids to navigation. Share that information with others on board and make sure someone other than you knows how to use the VHF to call for help.

A well prepared boat will allow you to concentrate on applying your seamanship to the task at hand. In all conditions, your primary focus should be on adjusting your speed to adapt to the conditions. There may be times when the safest and most comfortable speed is just fast enough to maintain control. It is also important to remember you may be essentially invisible to other vessels much of the time, since either you or they will be in a trough, below the line of sight. Enlist your passengers to help you keep watch for other boats and hazards in the water.

To the extent that you can generalize about such things, you can be faced with five basic sea conditions. As shown in Figure 22, they are: a *head* sea - where the waves are coming directly at your bow; a sea that is *broad on the bow* – coming at an angle between the bow and amidships; a *beam* sea – coming at a right angle to your keel; a *quartering* sea – coming at an angle between amidships and the stern; or a *following* sea – coming directly on your transom.

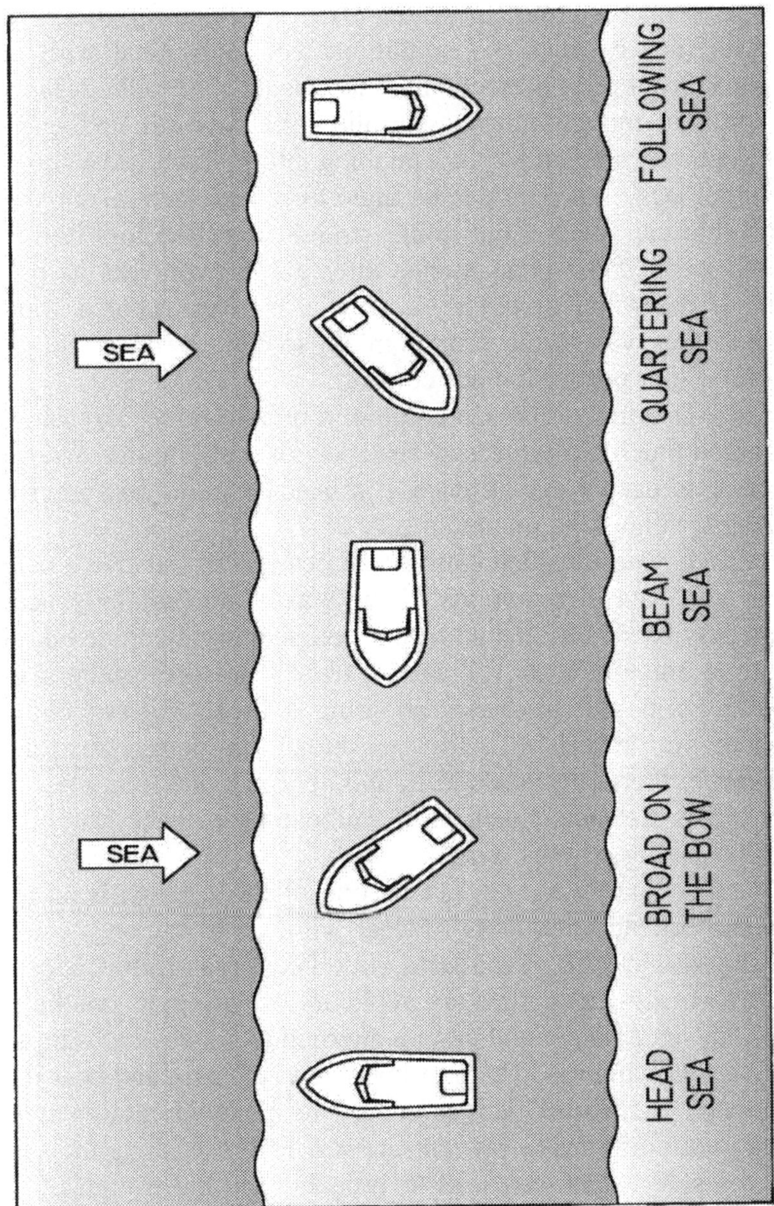

Figure 22

Boat positions vs. sea direction

Traveling into a head sea is the most comfortable of the possibilities because the conditions you must deal with are right in front of you. Secondly, most boats have been designed to provide enough buoyancy to allow the bow ride up the face of the next wave rather than pitching into it Each wave should be approached at a moderate angle to reduce stresses on your hull that can result from going straight over the top. Reduce your speed if the boat pounds after going over, lifts its prop out of the water or tends to bury its bow in the next wave. Remember, when your prop is in air, so is your rudder, so you have neither propulsion nor control.

Dealing with a sea coming in broad on the bow can be handled much the same as a head sea, except you may want to steer into each wave at more of a head-on angle as you cross to keep rolling to a minimum.

If your intended course requires you to travel in a beam sea, you have two options. If the waves are broadly spaced, you may be able to maintain your course and ride up and down with a minimum of rolling. In closely spaced, steep-sided waves, you will be better adopting a broad zig-zag course where you travel with the sea broad on your bow for a distance, then turn 90 degrees and accept a quartering sea for an equal distance, much as a sailboat tacks back and forth while beating into the wind.

A quartering sea can be one of the most difficult and uncomfortable conditions to deal with, as it not only causes rolling and yawing, but affects your steering as well. Choosing a broad, zig-zag course to avoid its effects may not be an option, since you would end up alternating between a beam sea and a following sea. The best approach is to grin and bear it, if you can. Remember, it is important to maintain enough speed in a quartering sea to prevent the wave from pushing the stern to the side, which can lead to broaching in the trough of the wave. Broaching is a very dangerous condition that can cause the boat to capsize.

A following sea is only slightly more comfortable, but requires more awareness and intervention to maintain a safe course. The severity of its effect is also determined, in part, by the design of your boat. A beamy craft with a wide transom will be more affected than a narrower boat with a deep-V bottom.

The dangers inherent in a following sea are:

1) It tends to propel the boat down the far side of a wave so stuffing the bow into the next wave is a possibility.

2) The sea may push the stern sideward and encourage a broaching situation.

Controlling the speed of the boat as it hurtles down the wave may require you to throttle back on power momentarily, while taking care not to lose control of the stern If you sense the stern is being pushed towards a broach, turn the wheel as far as possible in the direction the stern is heading and apply full power until the boat straightens The best strategy for negotiating a severe following sea - such as you may encounter going over a bar at an inlet – is to position the boat on the back side of a wave, just behind the crest and keep it there with careful throttle management until you get to calmer water. If you have trim tabs, you will present a smaller target to a following sea if you keep them retracted.

Navigating in heavy seas is a skill that must be learned through experience, because the conditions are never the same twice and every boat responds with its own handling characteristics. Maintaining your boat in good shape, knowing how to rig it for the rough stuff and having the basic knowledge of how to handle the helm will go a long way to insure a safe arrival at your destination.

Chapter 12
TRIM TABS

Powerboat trim tabs are metal flaps hinged at or near the trailing edge of a boat's hull. They can be tilted downward or drawn back up by a hydraulic cylinder or other mechanism whose action is controlled remotely from the helm Trim tabs are first cousins to ailerons, or wing flaps of an airplane. When the boat is under way, the tabs can be rotated down at an angle to provide increased lift at the stern - the greater the angle, the greater the lift.

The most common use for trim tabs is to correct the bow-up attitude caused by loading the boat too heavily at the stern or, more often, by the need or desire to go faster than displacement speed, but yet not fast enough to get up on plane Without the use of trim tabs, the boat is permanently "on the hump" - pushing a hill of water in the transitional attitude just before it goes on plane. Rotating the tabs down, as shown in Figure 23, will provide the lift needed to drop the bow and put the boat in a more manageable, safe and comfortable attitude while running at reduced speed.

The tabs can also be used to keep the bow down when heading into a chop. Without their use, a buoyant bow may try to ride up and over each wave, allowing the chop to slam on the bottom, making for a very rough ride and loss of directional stability. By deploying the tabs, the bow can be forced down so it knifes through the chop, rather than riding over it. Outboard motors and outdrives can be tilted down and in toward the transom to provide a similar effect, but the angle of adjustment is so small the effect is rarely as pronounced as it would be with trim tabs.

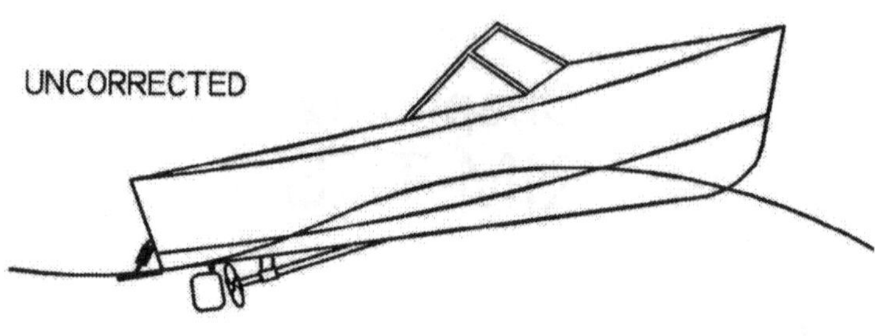

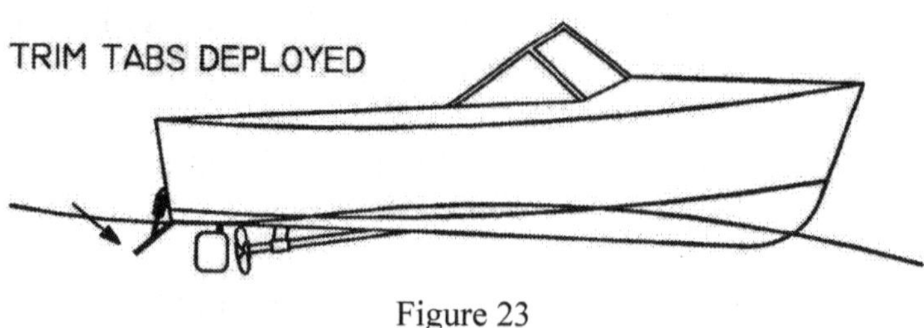

Figure 23

Using trim tabs to correct a bow-up running angle

Trim tabs have another important advantage - they can be operated independently to compensate for potentially dangerous side-to-side imbalances. Whether the list is caused by improper loading or by external conditions such as current or wind coming in on the beam, the tabs can be used to trim the boat back into a level attitude. As shown in Figure 24, a list to port can be trimmed out by lowering the port tab to increase lift on that side. (The downward travel of the tabs shown in Figures 23 and 24 is exaggerated for demonstration purposes.)

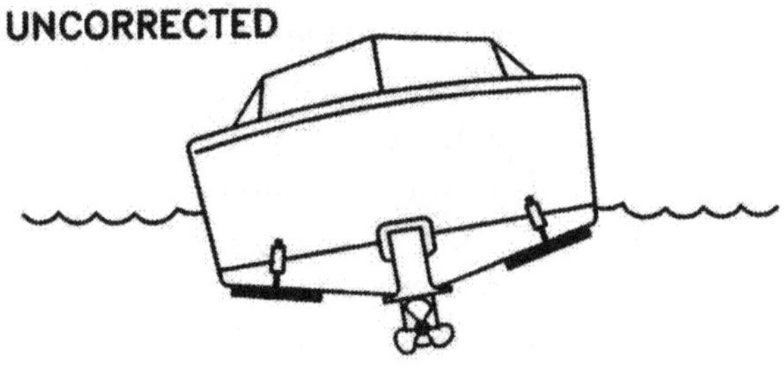

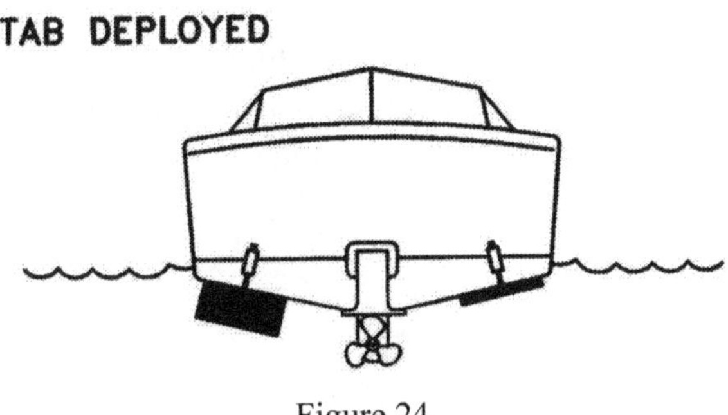

Figure 24

Using trim tabs to correct a list to port

The controls for trim tabs can be confusing and may require some concentration at first, but they soon become second nature. The confusion can come from the fact that the starboard switches control the port tab and vice versa To make matters worse, the actions of the controls are often labeled in terms of bow position, when you are thinking about the position of the stern. Getting the bow down requires you to raise the stern, so dropping the port bow means raising the starboard quarter.

Trim tabs are a very useful accessory, but they have some disadvantages. Using trim tabs to maintain fore-and-aft trim at intermediate speeds may mean that your boat is not being run in its most efficient manner. The resulting reduction in fuel economy can be made even worse by the drag the tabs produce - the greater the tab angle, the more drag In salt water, they are another piece of metal to factor into your electrolysis protection scheme If your boat has a swim platform, you will need to warn swimmers of the presence of the tabs to prevent injury from their sharp edges.

A more serious problem can arise from trying to back up with trim tabs deployed Their effect will be just the opposite of going forward. They will pull the stern down, make the boat plow into the water and impair your ability to steer In a worse case, a boat with a low or notched transom could even take on water in the process. It is important to remember to retract the tabs before reversing Finally, it is important to insure that tabs are fully retracted to prevent them from being damaged during launching or hauling operations.

Chapter 13
ANCHORING

Almost anyone who has spent an afternoon watching other boats in a busy anchorage can attest to the fact that a surprising number of boaters don't have a clue when it comes to setting an anchor. Time after time they drop their hook, only to have the boat drift off – dragging the anchor as it goes – until they luck out and snag something on the bottom or give up and leave. Much of their difficulty seems to stem from a lack of knowledge about how an anchor works and the conditions they have to set up to allow it to do its job

All anchors work alike. Most have some design feature, such as a crossbar or projection that is designed to roll them over (if necessary) once they hit the bottom, insuring their flukes are positioned to dig into the seabed. The flukes will only dig in if the pull of the rode is in line with the shank, not up or to the side. The only way to insure this will happen is to provide far more rode length than is required to reach the bottom. This means the boat ends up far away from the anchor site and is pulling laterally on the rode. (See Figure 25.) The extra rode is referred to as *scope*, which is measured as the ratio of its length to the depth of the water. One hundred feet of rode in twenty feet of water would equal a scope of 5:1. A scope of 3:1 or 4:1 is often sufficient for serene conditions, but 7:1 is the minimum recommended for windy or high current anchorages. When anchoring overnight a 10:1 scope is preferred.

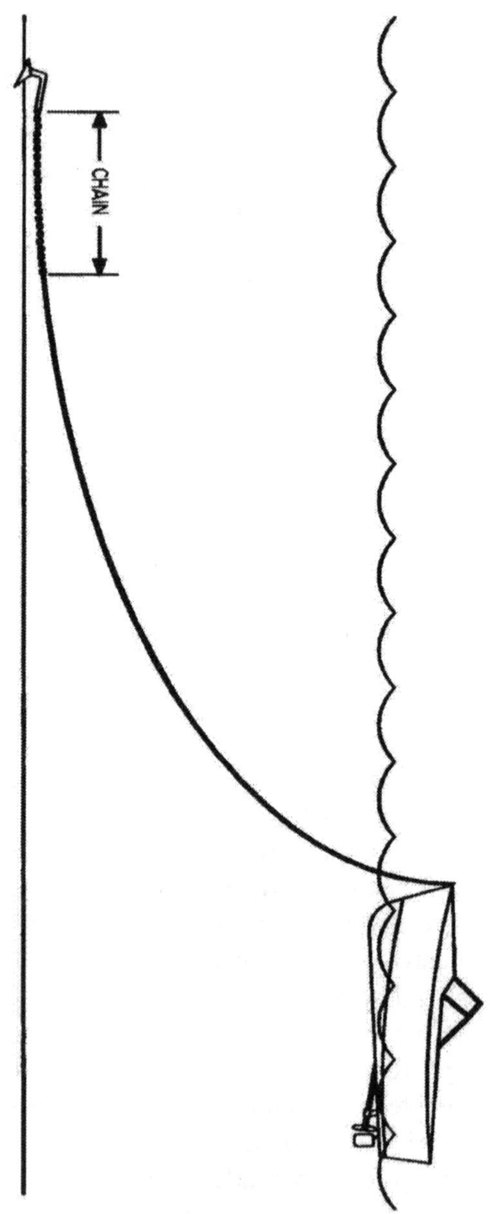

Figure 25

An anchor properly set using a 3:1 scope

The proper way of setting an anchor is to approach the site where the anchor will rest with the wind or current on your bow. Come to a stop, drop the anchor to the bottom and allow the boat to drift back in the wind or current until a proper amount of rode is deployed In the absence of wind or current, the boat can be backed down under idling power for the same effect. Once sufficient rode is paid out, set the anchor into the bottom by tying the rode to a cleat or bitt while the boat is still under way. The rode will come under tension and the motion of the boat will be arrested when the anchor is properly set.

The etiquette and practicality of anchoring dictate you check the position of any boats already there before choosing a site to anchor. Determine where their anchors lie and pick a site for yours that will avoid any possibility of entanglement with their ground tackle. Then insure your position will not encroach on other boats when you pay out sufficient rode to set the anchor. Be aware of the potential for swing when the wind or tide shifts and make sure the new position will present no danger.

If conditions do change and your boat swings to a different position, it may dislodge the anchor and reset it as the direction of pull changes It is important to have someone on watch in such an instance in case the anchor fails to reset The possibility can be avoided by setting two anchors, one forward and one aft, but make sure your aft anchor rode is well marked at the waterline with a fender or a buoy to warn other boaters of its presence so they know you will not swing when they do.
9191

Your ground tackle (anchor and the rode, consisting of chain and line) should be chosen carefully to match your boat, how you use it and the bottom conditions in the area you will frequent. Most anchor manufacturers publish charts which will allow you to choose the proper size for your boat Their recommendations will often include suggestions for the size and length of the chain portion of your rode as well A rode should always include at least six feet of chain Its weight helps position the anchor and its resistance to abrasion from rocks and debris on the bottom and also helps protect your ground tackle from wear and tear.

One of the most popular anchors for small boats is the Danforth type, which provides excellent holding in sand and mud. Its light weight and low cost make it a very popular choice, but it is not particularly suited to grassy, rocky or hard bottoms. For the latter conditions, most boaters will opt for a plow type anchor. They are considerably more expensive than the Danforth types, but are indispensable in rocky or hard-bottom conditions. Both types are shown in Figure 26.

Serious cruisers often carry both a Danforth and a plow, and prudent boaters always carry a spare anchor and rode. Even owners of small boats who have no intention of anchoring anywhere will find an anchor and a stout rode can be a very effective brake for a boat that has lost power and is drifting toward a dangerous destination.

Ground tackle can also serve as a useful tool if you run aground or find yourself in a situation where there is no room to maneuver or it would be dangerous to start your engine Tie your anchor to some floating object – a seat cushion or throwable PFD will do – and swim out with it as far from your boat as possible before untying it and dropping it to the bottom. Swim back to the boat and pull on the anchor rode to kedge the boat out into clear water. Avoid the temptation to emulate an Olympic hammer thrower by trying to heave the anchor out. Flying anchors can be deadly, and - unless you are a medalist in that sport – you will not achieve enough distance to be effective. Get wet.

One final caveat about rigging an anchor: Always check to see the rode is securely fastened to some point on the boat before deploying the anchor. Watching an unattached rode completely disappear over the bow to join your anchor on the bottom gives new meaning to the term “bitter end”.

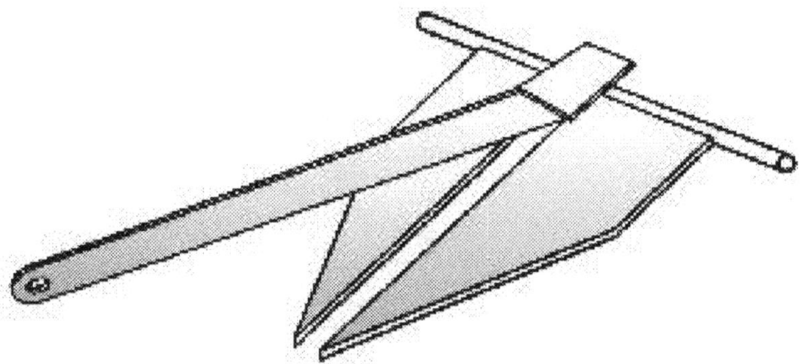

DANFORTH-TYPE ANCHOR

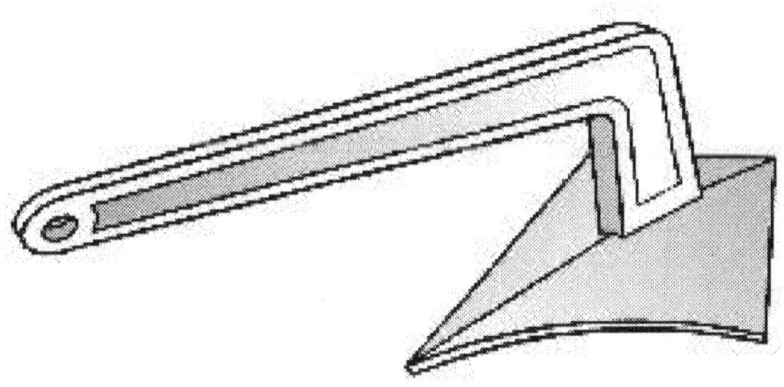

PLOW-TYPE ANCHOR

Figure 26

Chapter 14
DOCKHAND 101

Most skippers will readily admit to feeling uneasy about docking their boat, especially under adverse conditions like a strong wind or current They will also tell you that a sure cure for their anxiety is the sight of an able dockhand waiting to accept a thrown line and assist in the tie-up

The boating fraternity being what it is, people on the dock are usually more than willing to offer assistance This is especially true among people who keep their boats at a marina But all help is not created equal, and there are times when some peoples' help is worse than no help at all This chapter is written for the person on the dock, but it is information that you, the skipper, need to know, use and pass on to others as well.

If you are a prospective dockhand, you need to know the ropes - so to speak - and recognize that your responsibility doesn't end at simply catching a thrown line You need to look around and assess the docking conditions What is the wind direction and how will it affect the boat? Is there a current? And, if so, what is its impact? Are there people on the incoming boat who can help? How is the boat rigged? All of these are important to ascertain, because the assistance you provide has to match the situation at hand To make matters worse, sometimes your decisions will have to be made or modified at the last moment as conditions change.

An experienced skipper will provide some instructions as he or she approaches, letting you know which lines they will use and where they want them secured. If they are part of the permanent marina population or someone you may assist frequently, it makes sense to talk with them ahead of time so you know their preferences and habits. In either case, remember it is their boat and they are calling the shots. Unless there is a clear danger to life or property, you should follow their instructions, even if you "wouldn't do it that way".

The most important step is to get that first line established between the boat and the dock. The simple expedient of having one line secured can enable the skipper to use it as a spring line to control the position of the boat during the rest of the docking procedure. In most cases, the bow is the least controllable part of the boat in slow-speed maneuvers, so it makes sense to get it under control first. Once a bow line is secured, the skipper has the option of backing down or going forward on it as he maneuvers to bring the stern in. When the boat is finally positioned where the skipper wants it, the balance of the lines can be secured to the cleats.

There are as many docking situations as there are combinations of conditions. A common one is the need to use a stern line as the primary dockline when the boat is being pushed forward by wind or current. Bending a stern line to an aft dock cleat will help limit the forward motion of the boat and bring the stern closer to the dock. (See Figure 27.) A midships spring line can be used in the same way, but it may not be as effective as a stern line because it will not prevent the stern from swinging away from the dock.

A boat docking into a stiff wind or current may need to have its forward motion snubbed by using the bow line to take a purchase on an after cleat, then quickly switching the line to a forward cleat to keep the boat from being driven back. (See Figure 28.)

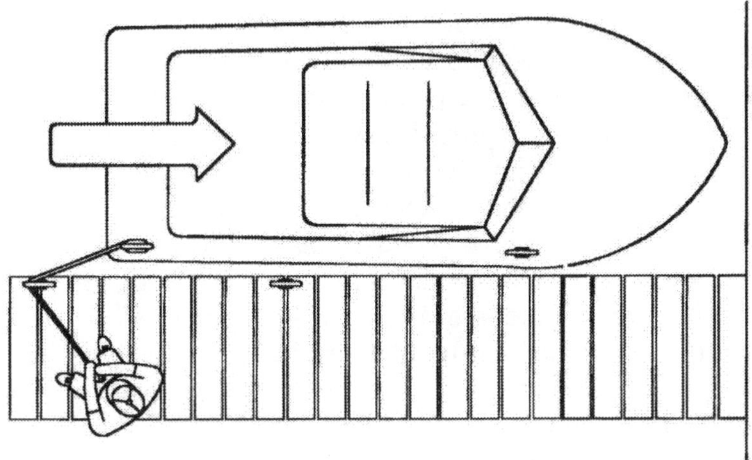

Figure 27

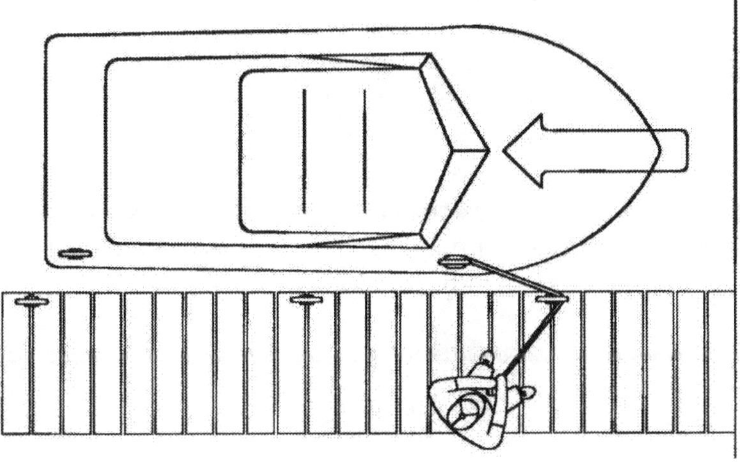

Figure 28

The proper ways to control the motion of a boat by taking a purchase on a cleat

One mistake nearly all inexperienced dockhands make is to hold onto the thrown line. They hold onto it rather than securing it to something substantial. If you can picture a 150-

pound person with a 2- or 3-ton boat on a leash, you understand the futility of such a stance. The first thing you should do when you receive a line is to make it fast to something – a cleat – a piling – anything solid In this case, *securing* or *making it fast* simply means taking a purchase – a half turn – around an object as shown in Figures 27 and 28. That half turn around a cleat can provide you with enough mechanical advantage to control the position of the boat or even stop its motion while still giving you the option of changing your purchase or providing some slack at the direction of the skipper. In all cases, keep the line taut, but do not make it fast until told to do so. For larger boats or more demanding conditions, a full turn around the cleat will more than double the effectiveness of your purchase. The ability to control the boat in this manner comes in handy if the current, an unexpected gust of wind or the boat's momentum is carrying it toward certain disaster.

It is a very comforting experience to watch the unruffled artistry of an able dock hand working to tie up your boat. While most of us have no intention of making it a career, we will be better off for having developed some knowledge and gained some experience in the subtleties of helping someone tie up uneventfully. A passing grade in Dockhand 101 will always come in handy.

Appendix A
GLOSSARY

abaft Toward the stern; behind.
abate To ease or desist.
abeam To the side, at right angles to the keel of a vessel.
aft Toward, at, in or close to the stern; behind.
amidships Midway between the bow and the stern.
ballast keel A blade-shaped projection suspended from the keel to place ballast below the hull.
beam 1. The width of a vessel at its widest point 2. A structural frame member athwartships, usually to support the deck or cabin sole; abeam.
bend To wrap or attach a line to take a purchase
berth A space at a wharf for a boat to dock -v. To bring a boat to dock.
bitt A heavy and firmly mounted device to which lines are secured.
bitter end The unfastened end of a line, chain or rode.
bow The front section of a vessel.
bow thruster A reversible, electrically or hydraulically powered propeller mounted in an athwartships tunnel just below the waterline at the bow; used to enhance slow-speed maneuverability by providing sidewards thrust during docking or turning.
buoy A tethered, floating aid to navigation -v. To keep afloat.
buoyancy The tendency to float in a liquid or in air.
chock A guide through which lines are led.
chop Closely spaced, wind-driven waves.

cleat A fitting, often in the shape of an anvil, to which lines are made fast

COLREGS (The International Regulations for Preventing Collisions at Sea, 1972) Rules of the nautical road governing vessels operating on the high seas Compare Inland Navigational Rules.

current The horizontal movement of air or water.

debark To get off a boat.

fender A cushion hung on the side of vessel to prevent contact with another object such as a dock or another vessel.

flemish To lay a line in a flat spiral for storage.

forefoot That part of the bow which is below the water line while at rest.

GPS (global positioning system) A navigation system which calculates and displays a precise determination of a receiver's geographical location using signals from a constellation of orbiting satellites.

ground tackle The complete anchoring system, including anchor, chain, rode and any buoys or trip lines.

helm 1. The wheel or tiller which steers a vessel 2. The control station.

Inland Navigational Rules Rules of the nautical road which regulate activities in harbors and certain navigable inland lakes, rivers and waterways.

jackshaft A driveshaft connecting a midships-mounted engine to an outdrive unit at the stern.

keel 1. The lowest fore-and-aft structural member of a hull 2. The central fore-and-aft ridge of a molded hull 3. A blade-shaped projection below the keel to counteract heeling under sail (also called a ballast keel).

launch A small, open boat used to ferry passengers -v. To place a vessel into the water.

lower unit The part of an outdrive unit or outboard motor which contains the propeller shaft and its drive gear.

make fast Attach securely; take a purchase.

marlinspike seamanship Skill in working with lines, splices and knots.

outboard 1. A motor attached to a vessel's transom or a bracket aft of the transom. 2. A boat so equipped. -adj. Positioned outside a vessel.

outdrive That portion of a stern drive abaft the transom consisting of a gearhead and the lower unit.

port The left side of a vessel when viewed from the stern -adv. Toward the left side. -adj. On the left side.

prop walk The paddlewheel effect of a rotating propeller, resulting in the tendency of a single-screw vessel to drift to the side, especially in reverse.

purchase An advantageous grip, hold or attachment to an object in preparation for using or moving it.

quarter The side of a vessel from amidships to the stern.

rode The line, cable, chain and fittings for an anchor.

rudder A pivoting blade suspended from or below the transom which can be turned from the helm to steer a vessel.

scope The ratio of the length of a rode or mooring line to the depth of the water. (Ex: 180 ft long rode in 30 ft of water = 6:1 scope)

secure To make fast; belay. (secure a line to a cleat)

single screw Having a single (inboard) engine which is connected to a propeller by a straight shaft.

skeg 1. An extension of the keel brought down and aft to the bottom of a rudder post to protect the rudder and the propeller. 2. A blade extending downward from an outboard motor or the lower unit of a stern drive to enhance steering effectiveness.

speed over ground The true speed of a vessel in traveling between two points, regardless of its speed through the water.

spring line A line other than the bow or stern line, leading forward or aft from its cleat.

starboard The right side of a vessel when viewed from the stern. -adj. On the right side. 101101-adv. To or toward the right side.

stern The aft section of a vessel.

stern drive An arrangement where the power from an aft-mounted engine is transmitted directly through the transom to an articulated outdrive unit on which the propeller is mounted.

strut A hanger, containing the Cutless® bearing, which supports an extended propeller shaft.

telltale A strip of fabric placed to detect and indicate air motion or wind direction.

transom The stern of a square-sterned boat.

twin screw Having two engines (and propellers).

warp To move a docked vessel by hauling on its lines.

wheel 1. A vessel's steering wheel. 2. The helm. 3. A propeller.

windage The amount of resistance to the wind presented by that part of a boat which is above the water line.

working part The load-bearing part of a line.

Appendix B
THE *VERY* UNOFFICIAL RULES OF THE ROAD

1. Know who has the "right of way".

Neither COLREGS nor the Inland Rules use the phrase "right of way" because there is no absolute right of way on the water. Instead, they use the terms "stand-on" and "give-way" to describe the responsibilities of vessels in situations where their paths may meet

The stand-on vessel should maintain its course and speed, while the give-way vessel is required to alter its course and speed to maintain a safe distance Being the stand-on vessel does not give you any rights. The rules are very clear that *all* vessels -- *including* the stand-on boat -- must take whatever evasive measures are necessary to avoid the possibility of a collision

There is a hierarchy in determining which vessel stands on and which gives way. If you are a powerboater, you end up near the bottom of the list, giving way to nearly everyone you meet. You are required to give way to boats being rowed, poled or pedaled, under sail, under tow, restricted by their draft or approaching you on your starboard bow. The latter is important. In a crossing situation, any vessel approaching you within an arc that begins on the centerline of your bow and sweeps 112 degrees starboard and aft (a point just aft of midships) is the stand-on vessel You must give way. When overtaking another boat, it is the stand-on vessel until you have passed, at which point the responsibilities are reversed – yours becomes the stand-on vessel and the other skipper must give way.

The above is an incomplete simplification of what you need to know. See Rule 8, below.

2. Be prepared.

Being prepared has many facets:

-Maintain your boat in a manner that insures it is safe and reliable.

-Insure that both you and the boat are properly equipped for the conditions you will face.

-Know what weather and sea conditions you will face before you leave the dock.

-Have a plan for emergencies and communicate it to your passengers.

Your failure to be prepared can mean inconvenience, injury or worse to you, your passengers, Coast Guard personnel, Harbormasters and other boaters who will have to bail you out when things go wrong.

3. Be responsible for your wake.

Your wake is capable of swamping small craft and causing severe damage to boats docked or moored nearby. Beyond the issue of courtesy to other boaters, remember you can be judged legally responsible for damage or injury caused by your wake.

4. Keep to the right.

Safety in tight channels and inlets requires courtesy and cooperation from everyone. You should be able to use half of the channel, but you are not entitled to take your half out of the middle.

5. Use the proper VHF channels.

Most marine VHF channels are restricted to commercial or government uses. Others have been set aside for specific, important purposes. Using them for frivolous chatting is inconsiderate and can be dangerous as well. Put yourself in the shoes of someone trying to issue a Mayday call or communicate with a rescue vessel before you use a reserved channel to discuss your dinner plans or ramble on about the fish you just lost.

Channels 9 and 16 are general hailing and distress channels, except in the Northeast, where 16 is restricted to emergency and distress calling only. Channels 68, 69, 71 and 72 are the recreational working channels. Channels 12 and 14 are set aside for port (Harbormaster, police and rescue) operations and 13 is used for communicating with bridges, tugs and certain commercial traffic. The latter three can be used by recreational boaters to contact those specific functions, but should not be used as working channels.

The proper way to use VHF radio is to make initial contact on the proper hailing channel in your area, then immediately switch to a working channel. If your conversation is going to last more than a minute or two, switch to a cell phone or finish it on a land line when you go ashore. There is precious little VHF space available – especially on a busy weekend - so we need to share the wealth.

6. Respect the rights and privacy of others.

Four fifths of the earth is covered by water. There is no need to blow past another boat just feet from its rub-rail or anchor within spitting distance of its swim platform. And remember that the folks in the next boat may prefer not to listen to your favorite rap artist at 110 decibels or inhale your exhaust for an hour while you charge up your batteries.

7. Practice the Golden Rule.

For the record, it is, "Do unto others as you would have them do unto you"; .....archaic, but it works.

8. Read the official rules.

You don't have to know them all by heart, but be

familiar with the ones that affect you. A paperback copy of *Handbook of the Nautical Rules of the Road* * takes up no room at all and should be aboard every boat (along with this one, we hope) for reference.

* Llana & Wisneskey; Naval Institute Press, Annapolis, Md. (ISBN 1-55750-504-7) Available through any bookseller.

PUBLICATION CREDITS

Parts of Chapter 11, "Handling Heavy Seas" were first published in *Trailer Boats* magazine. Reprinted courtesy of Poole Publications.

Parts of Chapter 12, "Trim Tabs" were first published in *Soundings*. Reprinted courtesy of *Soundings*.

Practical Seamanship
Written By David S. Yetman

Captain Jack's Basic Navigation
Written By Jack I. Davis

Creating Comfort Afloat
Written By Janet Groene

Living Aboard
Written By Janet Groene

Racing The Ice To Cape Horn
Written By Frank Guernsey & Cy Zoerner

Marine Weather Forecasting
Written By J. Frank Brumbaugh

Complete Guide To Gasoline Marine Engines
Written By John Fleming

Complete Guide To Outboard Engines
Written By John Fleming

Complete Guide To Diesel Marine Engines
Written By John Fleming

Trouble Shooting Gasoline Marine Engines
Written By John Fleming

Trailer Boats
Written By Alex Zidock

Skipper's Handbook
Written By Robert S. Grossman

White Squall - The Last Voyage Of Albatross
Written By Richard E. Langford

Cruising South
What to Expect Along The ICW
Written By Joan Healy

Electronics Aboard
Written By Stephen Fishman

Five Against The Sea
A True Story of Courage & Survival
Written By Ron Arias

Scuttlebutt
Seafaring History & Lore
Written By Captain John Guest USCG Ret.

Cruising The South Pacific
Written By Douglas Austin

Catch of The Day
How To Catch, Clean & Cook It
Written By Carla Johnson

VHF Marine Radio Handbook
Written By Mike Whitehead

REVIEWS

Trailer Boats
GOTTA HAVE IT
Brush Up On Boat Handling

How many boaters suffer embarrassment, or worse, due to lack of boat-handling experience? Anyone hanging around a marina or public dock for very long knows this is an all too common problem.

Now from Bristol Fashion Publications comes Practical Seamanship: How to Handle Your Boat Like a Pro, the latest book by Trailer Boats columnist David S. Yetman. This time the prolific author is out to help novice boaters gain mastery over powerboating -- and become better and safer boaters overall. According to Yetman, many boat-handling problems stem from inexperience and lack of familiarity with the mechanics of it.

Chock-full of basic information, the illustrated, 116-page book addresses issues pertinent to inboards with single or twin screws, outboards and sterndrives. Other chapters outline heavy-seas handling, docking and anchoring. This sturdy, laminated book is constructed to accompany you onboard.

Soundings
Practical advice for modern boaters

Bristol Fashion Publications is publishing two books by David S. Yetman this year.

"Modern Boatworks," (January 2001 $24.95) tries to

cover all aspects of the modern boat. It tackles the mechanical, electrical, communication and maintenance aspects of boating. Yetman also offers some do-it-yourself projects, such as customizing your instrument panel and resurrecting dinged propellers. The 244-page book is divided into 34 chapters, designed to promote browsing and easy access to the areas of modern boating that interest you most.

Yetman doesn't harbor any illusions about what his second release this year, "Practical Seamanship" (March 2001, $17.95), can manage in 116 pages. "The goal of 'Practical Seamanship' is not to make a bluewater cruiser out of every reader, but to provide the basics to help them handle their boats in a knowledgeable, responsible manner," writes Yetman in a press release.

Yetman breaks those basics down into straightforward chapters like maneuverability, External Influences, Docking, Handling Heavy Seas and The Very Unofficial Rules of the Road. There are plenty of simple, clear illustrations throughout the book to help the reader grasp the points. But as the author points out in the first chapter, only experience can help you truly master boathandling.

In both books, Yetman approaches each topic with a mix of experience, science and explanation that manages to be simple without being simplistic.

About The Author

Dave Yetman is a lifelong New Englander who's spent most of his adult life within sight of the water and comes by his nautical interests quite naturally. His seafaring ancestors include Labrador fishermen and lighthouse keepers and a Cape Cod grandfather who was an inventor and shipbuilder and noted for his models of historic New England lighthouses.

His own career has been in mechanical design and engineering, first as an entrepreneur and later as an engineering manager for an international technology company. He's been awarded patents for a wide range of devices, from motorcycle frames to biomedical laboratory instruments and enjoys applying his talents to his boats, which usually end up in a highly customized state.

His work has been widely published in the boating press and was recognized with awards in the 1997 and 1999 Boating Writers International writing competition. His articles, photography and technical illustrations have been published in *Boating World, Lakeland Boating, Motorboating, Offshore, Power & Motoryacht, Sail, Soundings, Trailer Boats* and *Yachting* magazines. He has three books to his credit, "The Boaters' Book of Nautical Terms", "Modern Boatworks" and "Practical Seamanship".

Dave and his wife, Pat enjoy cruising the New England coast on *CURMUDGEON*, their Albin Tournament Express convertible.

www.ingramcontent.com/pod-product-compliance
Lightning Source LLC
Chambersburg PA
CBHW022028090426
42739CB00006BA/332

* 9 7 8 1 8 9 2 2 1 6 3 7 3 *